GO GLOCAL

GO GLOCAL

THE DEFINITIVE GUIDE TO SUCCESS
IN ENTERING INTERNATIONAL MARKETS

CRAIG MAGINNESS

LIONCREST
PUBLISHING

GO GLOCAL

The Definitive Guide to Success in Entering International Markets

ISBN   978-1-5445-1053-8 *Hardcover*

978-1-5445-1033-0 *Paperback*

978-1-5445-1034-7 *Ebook*

To my wife, Ellen, my best friend and partner, whose love and dedication to our relationship and our family gave me the time and freedom to spend as much time traveling internationally as it took to learn the lessons that are captured in this book.

CONTENTS

INTRODUCTION

I suppose it was my curiosity that launched me headfirst into international business.

My journey began almost twenty-five years ago on a flight back from a business trip with the COO of our company. We enjoyed a candid working relationship, so as I listened to him air his frustrations about our struggling operation in Mexico, I was asking questions and making observations.

As he talked about our struggles, I was struck by how "American" our approach was with what was truly a Mexican company. This wasn't a maquiladora, a manufacturing operation on the Mexican border that exists to bring goods back to the United States. This company had its base of operations in Mexico City with a production plant in Tampico and served Mexican customers. Yet we operated as if the customers were Americans and played to those expectations.

I pointed out this disconnect to the COO. He paused for a moment to consider what I said before offering a response that changed the trajectory of my life.

"You should be the one running the operation in Mexico," he said.

"Me?" I laughed, sure he was kidding. "I've never even been to Mexico!"

"Craig," he deadpanned, "you can't screw it up any worse than we're screwing it up now."

Having no international business experience, I wasn't sure if that was true. But shortly after our initial conversation, I accepted a new position as the Director of Latin American Operations. My wife's reaction to the news showed how unexpected my entry was into the world of international business.

"Isn't there someone at the company who knows more about this than you do?"

Once in Mexico, I saw mistakes being made and worked to correct them. Along the way, I made plenty of mistakes myself. We acquired a second business in Mexico, began distributing in Uruguay and Argentina, and created a bigger penetration for the company in Mexico by bringing products in from the United States.

Things went surprisingly well for a guy with no experience. After our success in Mexico, I was tasked with turning around an equally challenging business we had in Italy. At the same time, I served as our company's supervising representative for a manufacturing joint venture we developed in China.

I'd started as a guy whose curiosity thrust him into uncharted waters, but since getting my start in Mexico, I've developed a passion for international business that I've carried throughout my career. I left the company in 2005 and now work as a consultant, educator, and public speaker. In 2013, I was honored to be named the Trade Educator of the Year by NASBITE International.

Looking back, it seems the COO had been right—I didn't screw it up.

Now I want to help you not screw it up with your international business endeavors.

YOU DON'T NEED TO GO IT ALONE

Many entrepreneurs, when they start a business, treat it like their baby. They love this idea they've brought to fruition with lots of sweat and tears and are understandably proud of their business and what it represents. They embody the timeless ideal of the self-made man or woman, and we applaud their tenacity.

But there's another side to this do-it-yourself approach that comes to light when owners try to tackle international business challenges all by themselves. Rather than use the resources at their disposal, they approach new problems as though they're the first person to ever face them. The go-it-alone approach may work in a familiar home market, but abroad, it's frequently the fastest path to a company's premature demise.

The other scenario is that people such as my younger self are put in new positions and must navigate their unfamiliar surroundings with limited experience. Companies aren't wrong to use international markets as opportunities to grow and develop promising talent, but they're taking the wrong approach if they don't equip their employees for success.

It's true that "business is business no matter where you do it" in the sense that you're using strategy and execution to earn a return on investment. But the context in which the business occurs has a huge effect on the right approach and the chances for success. If you want to succeed internationally, there is no one-size-fits-all approach.

In both cases, the key to not screwing things up internationally is to seek help when you need it and learn from the experience of others. That way, you avoid the obvious pitfalls that would sabotage your company's progress in a new market.

HELP ENSURE YOUR SUCCESS

If you're an entrepreneur, you can't go at it alone internationally; or if you're like I was and find yourself in unfamiliar territory, you have to learn quickly on the job. Luckily, there are numerous resources available that can make your life easier.

One that I'll recommend is your local World Trade Center. There are 319 World Trade Centers around the world that are part of the World Trade Centers Association and almost every major city has one.

Some, like one I've worked out of in Manila, are like executive office spaces you can use if you need a place to work while you're in town.

Others, like the World Trade Center Denver where I

served as president for a couple of years, offer training for companies of all sizes. We can help you with everything from international business and marketing strategies, to the nuts and bolts of how to do export documentation and regulatory compliance properly.

Another resource for American companies is the US Export Assistance Center (USEAC), run by the Department of Commerce and the Small Business Administration. Most major US cities have offices, and abroad, each US embassy has a senior commercial officer and a support staff that advocate for American business interests in that country. They're an excellent resource when you're considering an international venture.

For example, if I'm a business owner in Denver and I'm looking for a distributor in China, I can visit the local USEAC office and connect with the commercial officer's staff located where I'm looking to set up shop. The Denver office might also have an Asian market specialist who could prep me on taking my business to China.

Other government agencies also provide assistance. If you're in the food production industry, for example, the Department of Agriculture has offices in many foreign countries and can actually be more of an asset to you than the USEAC. At the local level, most states have offices for economic development with an international trade component.

THE WRONG APPROACH MAY PROVIDE A FALSE SENSE OF SUCCESS

At this point, you may be saying to yourself, "What can these offices provide me that I can't find myself? I meet people at trade shows and through industry contacts. Can't I partner with one of them?"

To answer that question, let me tell you a story about Tom, a small business owner whom I helped as a consultant, and how his experience with a Chinese distributor he met at a trade show went horribly wrong.

To hear Tom tell it, things started off smoothly. The two of them hit it off at the trade show and decided to work together to bring his product to a new market. Tom would visit the distributor in China, and on his way back from each trip, he'd write himself a memo detailing how the visit went. His first memo reflected an upbeat attitude as things got off to a wonderful start.

Coming back from his second trip, Tom's tone began to change. After traveling with a sales rep to visit customers, he began to think the distributor had been overselling the product. Things took a turn for the worse after the third visit, when Tom actively began using the word *negligent* to describe the distributor's behavior.

He worried that his product, which essentially allowed

pressure release in fluid flow manufacturing processes, could be installed incorrectly and cause an explosion.

After his fourth and fifth trips, Tom began to wonder if the distributor's behavior was criminal. He weighed whether to terminate their relationship. On his final trip, he couldn't locate the distributor or contact him.

When he visited a trade show, he found his original distributor's relatives selling a knockoff version of his product.

"I don't know why it was so difficult," Tom told me. "He seemed like the right guy when we met. How else are you supposed to find a Chinese distributor?"

Ignoring the fact that China has plenty of qualified engineers among its population of 1.3 billion, I asked Tom if he'd consulted with anyone at the USEAC office.

He had no idea what I was talking about.

"What about the World Trade Center?" I asked him.

"The World Trade Center?" he replied. "You mean the building in New York City?"

Tom assumed that because his small business had a couple of million dollars in sales annually in China, his approach was the right one. He was blazing a trail that—in his mind— nobody had ever blazed before. Had he consulted the local help that was available to him, he could've connected with a reliable Chinese distributor. Instead, he got a partner who knocked off his product and led to a messy legal action and even worse business situation.

Don't make the same mistake as Tom. Seek assistance before going international.

WHAT HAPPENED TO MYSPACE COULD HAPPEN TO YOUR SPACE

You need to carefully consider many factors before taking your business international. Sometimes subtle differences between cultures can cause businesses to fail just as quickly as those drastic, obvious differences.

Most of the time, when companies rush into new markets unprepared or select the wrong markets altogether, no amount of money can save them from failure.

MySpace provides a great example of a company that despite vast funding and resources, faced numerous challenges abroad because they underestimated the impact of cultural context on their success. That's not to say MySpace faded into obscurity due to their failures internationally, but that certainly was a contributing factor.

For those of you who've forgotten about the site (which is perhaps the point of the story), MySpace owned 75 percent of the US social networking market as recently as 2006. Facebook was second at 12.5 percent.

In 2005, MySpace was acquired by News Corp, Rupert Murdoch's global media conglomerate with roughly $30 billion in revenue and $62 billion in assets. News Corp made the acquisition because they saw that within a couple of years, the social media market was set to balloon from a $280-million industry to a multibillion-dollar industry.

If all MySpace did was maintain its market share, it would grow 400 percent in that time.

With the market leader in its pocket, News Corp embarked on an aggressive expansion of MySpace overseas. But instead of targeting areas where their product aligned with cultural values like it did in the United States, they saw the world as their new market. Given their domestic success, every country must be dying to have MySpace, right?

As it turned out, even their base assumption was wrong— companies elsewhere had also figured out social media and had established a foothold. Suddenly, MySpace wasn't the big player who owned the market; they were a well-funded startup trying to unseat competitors who had a massive head start in their new markets.

In the United Kingdom, for example, they were quickly eclipsed by Facebook, who targeted England as one of their first markets abroad and had left little room for MySpace when it arrived. In other markets, there were already homegrown social media sites gaining traction, and they were much more in tune with local cultural norms and tastes.

In Russia, MySpace saw a market where the number of internet users had exploded. What they didn't see was that the online advertising market that MySpace depended on for revenue hadn't matured there at the same rate it had in the United States, so the actual opportunity in that market was far smaller than they'd anticipated.

In non-English-speaking countries, the language barrier was a huge stumbling block, both in terms of the words on the site and the coding needed for such changes. The best example of this issue popped up in Israel, where the people not only spoke a different language, but read right to left instead of left to right. MySpace had to redesign its site infrastructure just to bring its product to customers in one small market.

Then the company ran into cultural issues that weren't readily apparent. The Japanese culture, for instance, values the group over the individual. A website that emphasized the individual as much as MySpace did was a total mismatch for their cultural values. Something as innocent as choosing your favorite bands or books on the site would be seen as differentiating yourself from your group identity and making it all about you.

In an effort to match those cultural values, MySpace tried to change its value proposition and became more like "OurSpace" in Japan. As we'll discuss in the next chapter, very rarely can a company change its value proposition to fit a new market and expect to succeed.

Countries in the Middle East, where relationships between men and women are policed differently than in the United States, also posed a significant challenge. If your product is built around the open exchange of ideas among all people, how can you expect to find traction in a country where that concept is more tightly regulated?

Unforeseen problems also popped up surrounding the complementary infrastructure that allowed MySpace to function, such as fast internet. Not every country MySpace went to had fast enough internet to support the site, which undermined the user experience. At the other end of the spectrum, South Korea had high-speed internet that already supported streaming video, so the MySpace experience underwhelmed users in that country.

It would've been crazy to say in 2006 that MySpace would

end up as a footnote in the annals of social media history, but their sloppy approach overseas combined with the ascension of Facebook sealed their fate. Now they exist as a *People/Entertainment Weekly*-owned entertainment site that caters primarily to musicians.

MySpace is also a sobering case study for small- and medium-sized businesses that can't afford to absorb the losses that News Corp did with MySpace. Because their margin for error is much thinner, they should learn from the mistakes MySpace made.

YOU MAY HAVE ONLY ONE CHANCE TO GET IT RIGHT

One of the lessons we can take from the MySpace example is that a surface-level understanding of the cultural context in your new market is not enough to establish business operations there. You need an intimate knowledge of the worldview held by customers there so you can determine how your value proposition might resonate.

This truth applies to businesses of all sizes. One of the amazing developments of the past decade is that thanks to the internet, the global marketplace is now accessible to even the small mom-and-pop operations doing business out of their garage or basement.

In my work as a consultant, I got to know a husband-and-wife team in Denver who sell baby carriers, and 70 percent of their sales are in Europe. Isn't that incredible? Of course, their success wouldn't be possible if they hadn't researched new markets, scouted out the competition, and focused on the market that was the best fit for their product and business. They took the appropriate steps to ensure they were not only filling a need for new customers but doing so in a way that was profitable for them as well.

It's a cliché to say business owners should think globally and act locally, but that's the mindset you must adopt in order to succeed. What we see as the global market is in fact thousands of local markets, each with its own set of cultural drivers that will dictate if your international venture is profitable or falls on its face.

If you fall on your face in a new market, that's probably the end of your opportunity there. MySpace didn't get a second chance to make a first impression in countries such as Israel and Russia. The former market leader gave users such an underwhelming experience that they could never recover against competition such as Facebook or more focused regional competitors.

There are exceptions to this rule, though. Global companies like Coca-Cola, Apple, and GE can have hundred-million-dollar mistakes in international markets and find success down the road with a new approach. Most small- and medium-sized businesses can't throw millions at the wall to see what sticks in a new market—it would destroy their existing business.

In that sense, you have one shot at going international with your business. You owe it to yourself to plan accordingly so you can get it right the first time.

Let's look at how this book will help you prepare for success.

A STEP-BY-STEP GUIDE TO ENTERING INTERNATIONAL MARKETS

This book has three sections, each detailing a phase of the process for going international—market selection, market readiness, and market penetration.

The following chart lays out the step-by-step process that will unfold in the pages to come.

GOING GLOCAL

STRATEGY →	TACTICS →	EXECUTION →
Market Selection	**Market Readiness**	**Market Penetration**
Value Proposition	Operations	Customer Development
Value Delivery	Marketing	• Making Contacts
Financial Drivers	Cust Service	• Cultural Acumen
Competitive Edge	Finance	• Alignment of Interests
	Legal	
	Human Resources	Business Structure
		• Exporting
		• JV's and WOFE's
		Delivery
		• Logistics, terms and Documentation

As you can see, this book will answer the big questions associated with each phase, which include:

- ✿ Market selection: There are approximately 195 countries in the world. How do you choose the right market(s) where you can find success?
- ✿ Market readiness: How will your company solve the logistical problems that arise from doing business abroad? How will this move impact your company culture?
- ✿ Market penetration: Once you've chosen your new market and you're confident your team is prepared, how do you enter the market in a way that will ensure you can make money in that market now and in the future?

If you're ready, let's dive into chapter 1 and consider the first question you must answer concerning market selection: Will my domestic success translate to a new market?

SECTION I

MARKET SELECTION: UNDERSTANDING AND REPLICATING SUCCESS IN NEW MARKETS

DOMESTIC SUCCESS: WILL IT TRANSLATE TO A NEW MARKET?

Based on the introduction, you might be tempted to think that the first step in taking your business international is examining the external factors that will hinder or bolster your chances of success: cultural factors, market size and opportunity, cost to seize the opportunity, and potential challenges you might face.

We will discuss these external factors in detail later in the book, because they are vital to your success in a new market, but that's not the starting point.

You actually want to begin a little closer to home by considering the factors that enable your domestic success.

It's imperative to begin this journey with a firm grasp on how your business operates and how it makes money here at home. After all, if you don't truly understand what makes your business tick, you'll struggle to replicate your success abroad and mitigate any challenges that pop up.

In this chapter, we'll examine the following four enablers of business success:

- Value proposition
- Core competency
- Financial structure
- Competitive environment

Let's begin with value proposition, or what makes your business unique.

KNOW YOUR VALUE

On its face, the term *value proposition* sounds like corporate jargon. I think part of the reason we roll our eyes when we hear this term is because we lack a definition that allows us to apply this concept to our business. Because your success abroad hinges on understanding your value proposition, let's define this concept.

Your value proposition is the story that you tell your customers. It almost doesn't matter what you sell, because people don't buy things based on characteristics such as speed or size. When people buy from you, it's because your product or service is part of a story that resonates with their worldview.

You can create loyal customers who are excited to buy from you when the story around your product or service—your value proposition—speaks to the personal truth of their worldview and how they project themselves in the world.

As you explore your value proposition, what you might find is that the story you're telling customers is not unique. When you find companies that are telling stories like yours, you'll discover your true competitors. These are the companies you'll have to fight for customers, not those that just happen to share your industry.

To explain what I mean, picture in your mind a Prius and a Hummer.

Both vehicles have two axles, four wheels, and an engine. They require the same complementary infrastructure—a network of roads, signs, traffic laws, and gas stations—and both are sold through a network of independent dealers.

Broadly speaking, a Prius and a Hummer compete in the same market space. People looking to buy a car, therefore, will consider factors such as gas mileage, cargo space, and safety features when choosing between these two vehicles.

But would you ever argue that a Prius and a Hummer are the same product?

Of course not. In fact, it's hard to imagine that a Prius owner and a Hummer owner could have a civil conversation about their choices in personal transportation.

Speaking generally, the Prius driver probably bought that vehicle because he believed his choice would have a positive impact on the environment by reducing his carbon footprint. Selecting a Prius reaffirms his worldview, and when he gets into his car in the morning, that choice is reinforced by how good he feels.

Conversely, the Hummer driver doesn't need to save the planet because she owns the planet. She feels like the biggest, baddest driver of the road, and it's that exhilarating feeling that caused her to buy the Hummer, not the features of the vehicle itself.

Even if you don't drive one of these vehicles, your perception of a Prius and a Hummer is impacted by how the value proposition of each one fits into your worldview.

Another great example of how we interpret value is found in bottled water.

In developed countries, water is an abundant resource that's essentially free. Gasoline, on the other hand, is a precious resource. In the United States, we freak out when the cost of a gallon of gas rises above four dollars. Yet, when you examine the cost of designer bottled water, people will happily pay ten dollars per gallon for something that's free from the tap.

Such a counterintuitive buying decision doesn't make sense until you examine the decision making that precedes the purchase. Customers will justify their purchase by saying the water is purer or has other benefits. In reality, they paid money for a free resource, because the story of that product aligns with their worldview.

These might be people who care deeply about what they put into their body. It's not enough for their water to be bottled, cheap, and convenient. They want to know, or at least hear a credible story about, where the water has been, who's touched it, and how long it's been stored.

The value proposition of your business needs to resonate with the worldview held by the customers you're trying to attract. The very idea of value or what is valuable is culturally determined. You cannot assume that just because you have a value proposition that resonates in your home country and culture that it will automatically translate to a new market with a different cultural orientation.

Take some time and reaffirm the value proposition of your business. Pay particular attention to elements of your story that are driven by your home country's cultural orientation. If you'd like to dig deeper into this idea of delivering value, I'd recommend Seth Godin's book, *All Marketers Are Liars (Tell Stories)*.

Once you're ready, let's examine how you consistently deliver that value.

DELIVER YOUR VALUE TO CUSTOMERS

If your value proposition is the "what" of your business, then your core competency is the "how." In this case, we're talking about how you deliver value to your customers. Being a successful company means doing many things right, but your core competency is the one thing you absolutely have to nail for your business to reach its full potential.

Chances are, your core competency falls into one or more of the following three categories:

- Manufacturing
- Sales/marketing/distribution
- Customer service

(There's a fourth category—capital allocation—but few businesses fit this type.)

Let's look at some examples of companies in the most popular categories for small- and medium-sized businesses: sales/marketing/distribution and customer service. I'll use a couple of big, well-known companies that you will recognize so you can appreciate the point.

Walmart is a classic example of a sales/marketing/distribution business. They aren't a manufacturing company, because they don't make anything themselves, and if you've ever visited Walmart, you're probably not raving about their customer service.

Walmart grew from a five-and-dime store in a small Arkansas town to a global behemoth thanks to their outstanding supply-chain management. They understand better than any other company how to get things from their suppliers into their stores and to their customers in the most efficient way possible. This core competency allows them to eliminate unnecessary costs and sell products more cheaply than their competitors.

That's how they deliver their value proposition of "every-day low prices."

If what you need to do to deliver value to your customers is to have intimate knowledge of and complete control over your supply chain, imagine the challenges you might face in taking your business to a new market where the customer and supplier data you rely on isn't available to you, or where the transportation infrastructure is too weak to support a consistent and timely delivery of your goods.

A fantastic example of a customer service company is Starbucks. Howard Schultz, the company's executive chairman, would be the first person to tell you that Starbucks doesn't actually sell coffee, but rather a community experience.

Starbucks wants you to feel welcomed when you come to their stores. That's why baristas are trained to learn your favorite drink order, each store has free Wi-Fi, and you're encouraged to stay and work as long as you like. If you know anything about the food service industry, Starbucks is one of the only companies that doesn't care how long you stay. In their mind, the longer you stay, the better.

It's almost beside the point that Starbucks sells coffee. In fact, back when people still bought music on CDs, Starbucks was the largest seller of music CDs in the United States.

Their value proposition is the feeling of community you get when you walk through their doors, that sense of returning home to something comfortable and familiar.

Top-notch customer service is the core competency they use to deliver that value.

Even if your value proposition resonates with the worldview of customers in your new market, you still must consider if you can successfully re-create your core competency.

For example, some cultures have a different idea of satisfactory customer service. Knowing a customer's name might be too intimate a relationship, or the community space like Starbucks provides might already be available in another context.

Furthermore, would you be able to hire, train, and retain the people needed to deliver your value proposition through the customer service experience? Employees who come to work in a different cultural context from our own could respond to incentives or their work environment in ways you wouldn't ordinarily anticipate based on your experience in your home market.

Even if you can replicate your core competency in a new market, can you make money while doing so? That's the next question we're going to consider.

MAKE MONEY, NOT SALES

Once you understand the value your business offers and how you deliver it, the next step is understanding how your company makes money. Can you explain how a sale at the top line of your profit and loss statement turns into profit at the bottom line?

This is where I see a lot of companies run into problems when they go international. Everyone gets excited about making sales in a new market and loses sight of the real goal, which is to earn an acceptable return on the company's investment. By focusing on new sales and revenue, they may be unaware of logistical challenges and unexpected costs that can undermine their ability to generate a good return.

After a few years, smaller companies in this situation will realize they're not making money, and they don't have a path to make money. For larger companies with the resources to adapt over time and begin generating a return on their investment, you'll often see decision makers pull the plug prematurely because the effort has been losing money or not performing up to expectations.

In many instances, desperate companies will chase sales to try and earn the return they need. They forget they're not in business to make sales but to make money.

The key to making money in this context, then, is understanding the financial structure of your business. The challenge is that not every company gets from the top line to the bottom line the same way. It helps to understand how the following equation applies to your company: *Velocity * Margin = Return on Investment.*

If you're generating an acceptable return domestically, you need to be able to replicate your margins and velocity abroad. If either variable goes down in your new market, the other must go up to maintain your return.

For example, some companies make a small margin on any given sale, but they generate high velocity. They earn a return on investment by quickly turning assets into sales. The challenge for this kind of company is that velocity can be hard to achieve if they're sending their products halfway around the world. The time from their plant to their new international market via an ocean freight ship could be four to eight weeks. Knowing this, a company dependent on high-velocity sales might consider a strategy that leads to a plant in their new market, which would keep their sales cycle short and their financial structure intact.

Another example is a company that provides high-level field service to drive a high margin. This company makes money by being on the ground and proactively solving customer problems as they arise. In the United States, it's no problem for their field service rep to travel from Cleveland down to Indiana, but what if that same rep now must go to India? That company would face many of the same problems as the high-velocity sales company: travel time, jet lag, time zone differences, and better local choices.

These companies have to consider if they can service their new market with their domestic staff or whether they should hire staff from their new market. Both routes pose challenges, but the latter option raises a whole new batch of questions, such as:

✿ Can I hire, train, and retain talented people in this market?
✿ How do I supervise and manage them?
✿ How does this approach affect my cost structure?

If you understand the financial structure of your business, you can plan for the likely challenges you'll face in bringing that structure to an international market. If you don't, and you're trying to fix issues as they arise, it's probably too late. International business success tends to follow a comprehensive, proactive approach.

STAY AHEAD OF YOUR COMPETITION

The final piece of this puzzle is understanding the competitive environment in your new market. If your business is a domestic success, it's probably because you know your competitors and how to stay ahead of them. But when you go international, you're a stranger in a strange land who must read and react to an unfamiliar landscape.

There might be competitors in your new market you've never heard of because they don't do business in your home country. In chapter 4, we'll look at the best ways to research your new market and discover these unknown quantities. The last thing you want is to enter a new region thinking you're the top dog when there's already a sophisticated company there from Germany or Taiwan that's way ahead of you in the market.

You'll also have to deal with local competitors that are already established and those that will create a knockoff version of your product and sell it for less. (Remember Tom?)

Competitors aren't the only factor worth considering in your new environment. You also need to analyze the forces at work that will influence your ability to be competitive. Porter's Five Forces is a great tool to use for this analysis. Michael Porter, a pioneer of modern strategic thinking and competitive dynamics, developed this analysis to help businesses address the less recognizable elements of their competitive environment, such as the regulatory landscape.

Regulations can provide a barrier to entry altogether. At

a minimum, complying with a new regulatory regime is likely to inflate your costs. Not only should you examine how regulations impact your costs, but also how they tend to favor local businesses.

Whether you use Porter's Five Forces to guide your analysis or some other tool, the important thing is to understand that your competitive environment includes factors beyond simply the other companies with which you compete directly. The following diagram summarizes the issues you will need to investigate to fully assess what allows you to be successful in your current market and how your competitive environment may change when you enter a new market abroad.

COMPETITIVE ENVIRONMENT

A SWOT analysis, which lays out the strengths, weaknesses, opportunities, and threats in a given situation, is another useful tool for analyzing how entering a new market will impact your competitive advantage.

SWOT ANALYSIS

STRENGTHS	WEAKNESSES
Expertise	Language Barriers
Intellectual Property	Long Distance Service
LEVERAGE STRENGTHS	MITIGATE WEAKNESSES
OPPORTUNITIES	**THREATS**
JV with Leading Marketer	Potential Competitors
Unmet Market Needs	Dilution of Resources
MOVE ON OPPORTUNITIES	PLAN FOR THREATS

If your business success depends in some way on patents or trademarks you hold, you'll want to research intellectual property law in the market you're considering. You'll need to refile those trademarks and patents, but in some countries, being able to set up and protect your intellectual property can be maddeningly difficult.

Even if you're able to file the paperwork, the practical protection of your property is another matter. Some business environments are lacking on the enforcement side, and the pirating of your intellectual property is a very real threat.

THE MOST CRITICAL ENABLER OF YOUR SUCCESS

Now that you recognize the four enablers of your success at home, the next step is identifying a market where you can replicate those conditions. Your value proposition is the most critical of these four enablers to identify and replicate abroad. If your value doesn't resonate with the worldview of potential customers in your new market, you're setting your company up for failure.

In fact, if you look at the other three enablers, they're all built around your value.

- ✿ Core competency: How do I deliver my value to customers?
- ✿ Financial structure: How do I generate profit from that value?
- ✿ Competitive environment: How can I leverage that value against my competitors?

Every international market you consider should be evaluated first and foremost by whether there are a sufficient number of people who share the worldview and the story that's encapsulated in your value proposition. As we'll see in a moment, if that's not the case, your chances of success drop significantly. In rare instances, companies can apply a secondary value proposition they don't focus on in their domestic market to create a resonance with customers in a foreign market.

For the most part, companies in that position will change their product or service to offer their value proposition in a way that does resonate in the new cultural context. A massive shift like this happens more often than shifting to a secondary value proposition, but it's time consuming and so cost prohibitive that usually only global brands can pull it off successfully.

If you're a small- or medium-sized business that's struggling with the question of whether your value proposition will resonate, the key to success is to go to a market where your existing value proposition will translate and resonate.

Once you've found one (or several), the next step is determining if your value proposition resonates with a significant demographic in that area. It's not enough to identify a value resonance in the abstract. You need to drill down and figure out the size of your actual market in that area. Finding this kind of sizable market opportunity is fundamental to proactive market selection, which we'll look at in the next chapter. You're trying to answer the question: Is it worth my company's time and resources to pursue this new opportunity?

With that said, let's look at two global companies that took diametrically different approaches to this part of the process.

TWO CASE STUDIES IN TRANSLATING VALUE: CAMPBELL'S SOUP AND OREO COOKIES

In 2007, Campbell Soup Company began to study potential markets for international expansion. What they discovered was that Russia consumes more soup per capita than any country besides China, which made it an easy target market for their expansion. Knowing this, Campbell's updated its products for a new audience and set out to conquer the Russian soup market. It seemed like a perfect match.

Despite their initial optimism, the company exited the Russian market in 2011 and took a multimillion-dollar write-off on their failed investment in the country.

The mistake Campbell's made was believing their value proposition was soup when, in fact, they don't sell soup any more than Starbucks sells coffee. The company's value is convenience, that ability for parents to come home after a long day of work and get something on the stovetop that feeds their kids and fills the kitchen with the wonderful smell of soup (like grandma used to make) with none of the work.

We all love that feeling of warmth and goodness that soup gives us, and Campbell's allows its customers to experience that feeling in a few minutes.

In Russia, soup is experienced in a different cultural

context. Russians enjoy soup because of the preparation—going to the marketplace to find ingredients, cooking at home with different generations of their family, enjoying conversations, and making those family connections that life is all about. The idea of undercutting that emotional experience for convenience was anathema to most Russians.

That's not to say there weren't busy people in Russia who bought Campbell's soup, but it wasn't a large enough demographic to justify the company's investment in that market.

In Campbell's defense, they did their homework in Russia. For example, they hired cultural anthropologists during the market research phase to interview Russians about soup; however, their application of that data was a classic example of confirmation bias. The company had its sights set on Russia, so when they heard quotes like "Soup is like my grandchildren," it only confirmed their belief that Campbell's soup was perfect for the Russian market.

In actuality, the Russian people were saying that soup was about family for them. It's like their grandchildren in that they invest time in it and share it with others.

Campbell's soup didn't fit the Russian culture at all, so their efforts there flopped.

Kraft Foods took a different approach with its Oreo cookie brand in China. Since first being introduced in 1912, Oreo has become the best-selling snack cookie in the United States. Given its domestic dominance, it seemed like a natural fit for Oreo to expand internationally when the Chinese market opened up in the 1990s. After all, who wouldn't want to experience the joy of dunking an Oreo in a glass of milk?

As it turns out, the Chinese people didn't. Oreo hit the Chinese market in 1996 and encountered roadblocks right away. These new customers didn't like the sweetness and texture of the Oreo; plus, their perception of value was different with regard to how many cookies should come in a package.

Oreo could have done what Campbell's did and exit the market. Instead, they took a step back after a decade of struggle and considered how they could deliver their value proposition in the context of the Chinese culture.

Like Campbell's and Starbucks, the value Oreo delivered wasn't two chocolate wafers with white cream in the middle—it was the small guilty pleasure of eating something sweet that makes you happy.

Their value proposition resonated with the Chinese people, just not in the way it was currently being delivered through their product. The solution was to redesign the Oreo cookie to suit the tastes of their new customers. The wafers and familiar white cream were replaced with what is essentially a chocolate-dipped straw.

The company also redesigned its packaging to better fit the Chinese culture, while also retaining its signature Oreo look. Both efforts symbolized the perfect marriage of a company's values and the cultural values of a new international market.

It paid off, too, as Oreo is now the best-selling snack cookie in China.

We can glean two main takeaways from studying Campbell's and Oreo:

✿ If global companies can spend millions researching a new international market and still encounter challenges that cause them to fail, it can happen to any business.
✿ Kraft had the money to redesign its Oreo product line after initially failing to gain the traction they expected in China. Most small- and medium-sized businesses don't have that luxury.

The goal, therefore, should be to select the right market for your business, minimizing the cost that challenges impose, and avoiding the damage they can wreak on your existing business. There is no such thing as a frictionless entry in an international market, but if you take a proactive approach, you can make the experience as painless and profitable as possible. Let's look at how you can select the right market for your business.

CHAPTER 2

WHERE: THE RIGHT FOREIGN MARKET AND PROACTIVE MARKET SELECTION

If I had to put a number on it, I'd estimate that 80 percent of companies that wind up in the wrong market got there by reacting to an external factor. Rather than proactively researching new market opportunities, they overreact to chance encounters.

Let's look at a couple of examples. Almost every business has a website with a contact form that anyone in the world can access. When a reactionary company receives an inquiry from someone in Thailand who wants to buy their product, instead of doing their due diligence, they start thinking about new sales in Thailand.

Fast forward a year and now they're in a market where their value proposition may not resonate, but by the time they learn that, it'll likely be too late to save things.

Remember Tom's chance encounter with a Chinese distributor at a trade show? He got swept up in the allure of overseas sales and rushed into a bad business relationship. You see the same thing happen to a lot of businesspeople at trade shows—they meet someone who wants to sell their product in Chile, for example, and after a few emails and meetings, they have a half-baked operation in Chile.

Marketing and sales staff can also get stars in their eyes after learning through their network that their rival has 30 percent of their sales in Taiwan. The C-suite folks are miffed when they hear this "intel" because the competition is doing well in Taiwan and they're not even in the market. Pride and jealousy might push them into a potentially bad market. However, if they'd stopped and considered the following facts, they might have gone to a different area:

- ✿ "Intel" from competitors isn't always reliable. And salespeople never exaggerate, right?
- ✿ An international market that works for your competitor might be a total mismatch for you. That's assuming your competitor actually did their research and made a good decision entering that market.

✿ Your competitor's actions shouldn't dictate your strategic decision making.

The key to choosing the right market is a proactive approach. If you choose to develop international sales, do it on terms that are strategically advantageous to your company. You want to select markets where you have the highest probability of success, as opposed to winding up in markets due to random external factors.

As you examine potential markets, there are three main criteria to consider.

WHAT'S THE SIZE OF YOUR OPPORTUNITY?

When you're evaluating new markets, the first criteria is the size of your opportunity. Specifically, you need three things:

1. People
2. People with money
3. People with money who can become your customer (i.e., people with a worldview that resonates with your value proposition)

Are there enough people in this potential market to achieve the kind of market penetration you need to be profitable? Furthermore, consider how those people are spread out over their geographic region. A lot of people spread out over a large area with insufficient infrastructure connecting them may be less attractive than a smaller number of people concentrated into a single geographic area, like a large city. Shanghai, for example, might be a better market than a country with twenty million people spread out over a large area.

The next step is to find people with money. You might start with gross domestic product (GDP) to see how much money is in the overall economy. This metric is useful, but it doesn't necessarily indicate that people have money. In some countries with a high GDP, the money is concentrated in a small percentage of elite, while the rest of the country is uniformly poor.

If you're selling a consumer product or service, you need people with disposable income, not just a country with a high GDP. One metric you should consider is consumer credit as a percentage of GDP. There's a strong correlation between the development of a middle-class consumer market and the extension of consumer credit for credit cards, car loans, mortgages, and more.

When consumers in a heavily populated area have the need for your product plus the means to buy it, that can represent a sizable opportunity for your business.

This assumes you've found a market where these people who have money are likely to be your customers, which gets back to how well your value proposition resonates with their worldview. There are a few ways to validate this assumption, starting with statistics about the market size and growth rate for your product.

The United States uses the Harmonized System (HS) for tracking the import and export of goods. You can use that information to see if your potential market is importing goods in your category, which would indicate enough of a demand to justify an import market. The way these data are categorized can get murky at times, making it hard to find products similar to yours. You might also find your product isn't being imported into your prospective market at all, which isn't necessarily a bad thing. In these instances, look for products with a similar value proposition.

For example, I worked with a company years ago that sold a high-end line of skin care products mainly to aesthetician spas, which was too granular a niche for us to find market data. Instead of looking at skin care products, we focused on purchase data for designer bottled water such as Evian and Perrier. We felt the popularity of those products reflected a desire for high-end personal care products like ours.

In a market where you don't see a huge match, there might still be a niche market for your product. If you can find one million people among China's population of 1.3 billion who will become your customers, that could be worth pursuing. You just need to adjust your expectations and plan accordingly with niche markets.

WHAT ARE THE DIRECT AND INDIRECT COSTS OF ENTERING THAT MARKET?

The second criteria to consider is the cost to access the opportunity you find, which breaks down into two categories: direct and indirect costs.

Here are examples of direct costs your company might incur:

- Packaging and shipping
- Compliance testing and certification
- Manufacturing/design changes
- Foreign-language materials
- Service and support personnel
- Travel
- Legal compliance/intellectual property protection

Some of these direct costs, like shipping or travel, are more obvious than ones like foreign-language materials. If you've never done business internationally before, an easy assumption to make is that everyone speaks English and you can ship your marketing materials over there without making any changes.

While "international business English" is spoken around the world, idiomatic English can be easily misunderstood, thus necessitating translation of your materials into the language of your new market and the cost associated with that process. (We'll discuss this in more detail in chapter 5.)

We've discussed regulatory compliance, but there are direct costs that come from hiring new personnel you might need for this process: a freight forwarder, a lawyer who understands consumer protection regulations, or a banker with foreign exchange experience, just to name a few examples.

Indirect costs can come from a distraction of resources as you shift money, time, and manpower away from current endeavors to pursue a new opportunity. There's also the cost of training your existing staff to handle customers whose cultural context is different from theirs. In addition, you might have to train foreign sales reps to understand your value proposition and the products or services you offer. The challenge is working with people who speak English as a second language, meaning your existing training materials might not be sufficient for properly training them.

Because many small- and medium-sized businesses can't afford to immediately hire a full-time person to focus on their international interests, they must also incur the indirect cost of pulling someone away from their regular job duties to head up that charge. (In chapter 6, we'll look at the qualities a person in this role should have.)

WHAT IS YOUR PROBABILITY OF SUCCESS?

Once you understand the size of your market and the costs involved, there are still a host of other complexities that will affect your probability of success. This is a good time to revisit the risks you identified using your competitive environment analysis. Consider any barriers to entry you might face, such as:

- How transparent is the legal system in your new market?
- If you need to hire employees, how accessible is the labor force?
- If the labor force is accessible, is the level of education sufficient?
- Are the government and currency stable? Will they be in the future?

The level of both current and potential competition is also a critical consideration. The size of the market may not reveal how saturated it is with competitors whose value propositions are similar to yours. Is there room for a new player in this market? If there is, what are the attitudes of customers toward substitutes for existing domestic options?

Half the battle when you're trying to succeed in a new market is mitigating risk, which is why market selection is not just about size and cost. Even if a market has a sufficient number of customers and can be accessed at a reasonable cost, you should avoid it if there are significant risks present that can't be managed or mitigated through intentional and proactive planning.

The risks that are present that can be managed need to be accounted for in your company's plan. If you fail to address these risks, your business might end up chasing sales instead of earning an acceptable return on your investment, which will ultimately lead to failure. In order to replicate the four enablers of your domestic success—value proposition, core competency, financial structure, and competitive environment—in your new market, you need to address risks up front.

With those three criteria in mind—size, cost, and probability of success—let's assess some popular international markets.

WHAT ARE THE BIGGEST INTERNATIONAL MARKETS?

Depending on who's counting, there are approximately 195 countries in the world. If you look at the sum of the GDP for every country, almost 70 percent of the global economic activity comes from the twenty largest markets, which include the United States, the European Union (EU), China, and Japan. Let's exclude the United States and focus on the activity happening in the EU, China, and Japan, because these markets provide an attractive entry point for many international ventures simply due to the size of their economies.

If you look at the EU as one market, it's roughly the same size as the United States. As of this writing, both markets produce about $18 trillion in economic activity. China is close but still well behind at about $12 trillion, while Japan is a distant fourth at about $5 trillion. The fact that these handful of markets represent the majority of the world's economic activity is the Pareto principle in action—the vast majority of the world's money is found in a small percentage of countries.

Don't overcomplicate things in your search for an international market. The goal of a business is to make money, so follow the money.

That's not to say there aren't compelling reasons to

look outside the top twenty markets. If your company is involved with infrastructure development, clean water projects, or delivering power to rural areas, look at developing markets in Africa where the consumer base is less important than government expenditures on these types of projects.

Here's another example. You might run a US business but have existing connections in a South American market where there's an affinity for your product or service. If you evaluate that market against the criteria we've looked at and find it's a good match, that's a perfectly legitimate reason to enter a market outside the top twenty.

THE FOUR LEVELS OF THE MARKET

As you research developed markets across the globe, keep in mind there are actually four levels of the market: global, glocal, local, and needs-based.

I came across this concept while reading an article in the October 2006 edition of the *Harvard Business Review* and loved it. The author's argument was that four levels of the market exist within developing economies. It starts with the global level, where products and services conform to global standards, and pricing is global as well. It's mainly the major corporations that do business at this level.

At the opposite end of the market is the needs-based level where necessities are subsidized or purchased through government programs. Think about Africa, where a major opportunity for companies is government demand for needs-based goods.

In between these ends of the spectrum are the glocal and local levels.

At the glocal level, global products face competition from locally available substitutes. As a result, products may be manufactured to fit with local tastes and priced differently to both meet cultural expectations and stay competitive with the local alternatives.

Below that is the local level where product features and pricing are decided by the companies and customers in that economy, not global standards.

If you think about the levels of the market like a pyramid, the smallest level—the point of the pyramid—in developing economies is the global level. At the base, the needs-based level is the largest, with the glocal and local levels in between. In developed economies, the pyramid is inverted so that the global level at the top now makes up the largest level, while the needs-based level is the smallest.

Understanding each level allows you to find your opportunity in the market, see how you stack up against the competition, and understand how your product and pricing might need to change. While companies like Apple compete at the global level, most small- and medium-sized businesses need to look for openings at the glocal and local levels.

Being able to excel at these levels requires companies be attuned to the culture of their new market. You can't do that from afar; you must be on the ground so you can begin to learn local tastes and preferences. These insights will drive how your product looks, how it's packaged, and what you can charge for it. A mistake many companies make is assuming their domestic pricing will apply in an international market. As we've seen, what works at home won't necessarily work abroad.

To better enable your proactive market selection, let's dive deeper into the market dynamics in China, the EU, and Japan, and learn more about expectations in each area. For US companies, we'll also take a look at our North American Free Trade Agreement partners, Mexico and Canada.

CHAPTER 3

UNDERSTANDING THE MAJOR MARKETS

Each of the three biggest markets outside the United States—China, the EU, and Japan—present ample opportunities for businesses to expand internationally. However, each market comes with its own set of challenges that aren't always apparent from a macro-viewpoint.

As we saw with Campbell's Soup, what seems like a perfect fit can be a total mismatch if you don't take the time to learn about the nuances of your potential market. What seem like small details can be significant enough to derail your success if you ignore them.

With that in mind, let's explore the markets in China, the EU, and Japan in more detail to see what obstacles you might encounter as you pursue new opportunities. We'll start with China, which is undeniably an appealing option for many businesses right now.

THE MIRACLE OF THE CHINESE ECONOMY: CHALLENGES AND OPPORTUNITIES

The main reason China is such an enticing international market is that it's home to 1.3 billion people, roughly four times the population of the United States. Coupled with its explosive economic growth over the last twenty-five years, China seems full of opportunity. This new status quo is actually a return to normalcy for a country that up until about 150 years ago was arguably the most technologically advanced, leading economy on the planet.

It was only from about the mid- to late 1800s through the 1900s that China became an impoverished, developing country. I witnessed this firsthand when I first visited China in the mid-1990s, not too long after Deng Xiaoping's economic reforms had begun to take effect nationwide. The middle-class consumer market was about one hundred million people—not a bad size but spread out over a large area with an underdeveloped infrastructure.

On the streets of Shanghai, where we were staying, you'd see mostly bicycles and the occasional Mercedes. About fifteen minutes outside the city, the road turned to gravel, then dirt. Getting from there to our next destination, the city of Changzhou, involved a three-hour ride over a dirt road, surrounded by animal-pulled carts and retrofitted rototillers. We arrived at a gray, concrete, industrial city.

I've returned to China many times over the past twenty-five years and was there recently. Today, the middle-class consumer market is roughly eight hundred million people. The trip from Shanghai to Changzhou now mostly takes place on a high-speed, six-lane interstate. It's also one of the stops on the comfortable, efficient bullet train that runs from Shanghai to Beijing.

The physical signs of progress are immediately evident and very impressive, but what's truly amazing is the way China has raised about seven hundred million people from abject poverty to the middle class in just twenty-five years. It's an economic miracle that was accomplished through perhaps the most effective antipoverty program in human history. By allowing a mostly competitive, largely capitalistic economy, China has regained its standing as a global superpower despite their political system (which we'll discuss in a moment).

It can be tempting to observe this progress and think, "We've got to get to China—that's where the action is!" But before you hop the next plane to Shanghai, let's examine some downsides of the Chinese market that have diminished its appeal in recent years.

Over the last twenty-five years, China hasn't just experienced economic growth; they've essentially undergone the industrial revolution that Western markets underwent for two hundred years. When the Chinese first opened their market internationally, consumers would buy anything Americans made, because they needed everything to get the economy going. Today, China's manufacturing capacity is exponentially more developed.

The Chinese can make almost anything they want now, and not only that, they'll make it cheaper in their local market. Like many other parts of the world, there is a degree of protectionism and nationalism within the Chinese economy that didn't exist two decades ago. Their economy is developing with that principle in mind, which means fewer opportunities for foreign companies looking to do business in Chinese markets.

Not only are economic attitudes changing, but China now faces critical structural issues that could prevent them from sustaining their unparalleled progress.

One issue is that as China's rapid economic growth begins to slow down, it creates more and more political tension within the economy. There's a real question, even in the minds of party leaders, about what will happen to the Communist Party's power when the growth level slows down to the global norm for a developed country. I have spoken with people who are genuinely concerned that if annual GDP growth slows to a rate of 3 percent or less, there will be wide-scale civil unrest and political upheaval.

Another issue is the real estate bubble China now faces. If you travel to any large city, you'll see blocks of skyscrapers covered in green netting and cranes wherever you look. Despite massive construction projects in the major cities, many of the new buildings are empty.

Opportunities for private Chinese investors are somewhat limited, so many investors pour money into real estate. It's a great investment as long as there's demand, but right now there are more empty buildings than there is demand. If the value of this real estate were adjusted to reflect its market worth, China could face an economic calamity.

By condensing a two-hundred-year industrial revolution into twenty-five years, China now faces some well-documented environmental challenges. The Chinese people traded their quality of living for explosive economic growth, and now they're paying the price for that decision.

We hear a lot about clean air issues in Beijing and other large cities in China. Having been there over the years, I can personally say it's a real issue. The industrial base still uses a lot of coal, plus there's been a huge increase in the number of privately owned automobiles on the street. I have been in Beijing on the rare beautiful, sunny day, but I've also been there on days when you could barely see across the street. The air quality is extremely poor, and the government has a hard time controlling it.

There's an even bigger issue than air pollution, although you don't hear quite so much about it—access to clean water. As you travel across China, you'll see many green, stagnant estuaries, which explains why many of the Chinese people I know won't drink local tap water. I know people who've gotten fairly serious skin issues simply from showering in the water, particularly outside of the major cities. I've also read stories about elevated cancer rates in smaller towns. This news has led to civil unrest among people in those areas, but of course, news of this unrest is quickly suppressed by the government.

With the rapid growth of a middle-class consumer market, you have more people with a substantial and legitimate interest in political outcomes and the results of government policies. Clean air and water are among the things that people in a developed middle-class economy want and demand from their leaders. The Chinese government is under far more scrutiny than they have ever been. As a result, these environmental problems are finally being recognized, and money is being set aside to mitigate them.

That said, China is very close to a tipping point. What happens when citizens don't have sufficient clean air and water? In addition to the possible political or violent reactions from the middle class, these shortages would reverberate throughout the economy.

The government is directly responsible for the last major challenge in the Chinese market: moving from an industrial age economy to an information age economy. There is no vibrant and free flow of information in the Chinese economy. Information is tightly controlled by the government, which uses censorship to maintain political control. As a result, China is struggling to step fully into the digital world we now inhabit.

Billion-dollar companies like Facebook and Google have had difficulty making inroads in China, because the government has blocked consumers from using their products and services. As technology becomes more infused with our daily lives, China is falling further behind the other leading economies of the world that have leveraged the information age to improve the lives of their citizens and grow their GDP. Startups and entrepreneurs in China face an uphill battle in creating information-based products and services when the free flow of information itself is suppressed.

If the value proposition of your company revolves around

the free flow of information—like MySpace did—then China probably isn't the right market for you, because you'd likely struggle to deliver that value. The Chinese need to make this critical market transition to continue their economic growth, but until they do, I'd look for a better fit.

There are still some excellent opportunities to expand into the Chinese market despite these limitations, starting with high-level technology. When it comes to things like industrial equipment, if the Chinese need it, they can make it. But most of their domestic tech is copied from technology from other countries. This is especially true regarding the high-tech systems on which many lives depend—rather than build it in China, they'd prefer to look at a technology developed and tested in another market.

For example, the bullet trains I mentioned earlier are made in France. While the Chinese do produce airplanes and airplane parts, the critical aerospace controls that go into them are mostly imported. Some of this is due to technological capabilities, but I also think the sense of an underlying level of corruption within the Chinese economy plays a part.

The second major area of potential in the Chinese market is cultural artifacts. These are things that the Chinese can't make because they're unique to other places. Currently, for example, there is a huge demand in China for American movies. American clothing companies are also doing very well, as are American automobiles.

Even Starbucks is successful in China, not because of a demand for decent coffee, but because Starbucks itself is a cultural icon. For a middle-class Chinese person, to be able to carry around a four-dollar cup of coffee from this famous brand is a status symbol. It shows that you have arrived; you're living the American dream, now the Chinese dream.

For most of us, China is a large and unfamiliar place with an inaccessible language. It can seem daunting to travel there, let alone try to do business. The first thing I would suggest for anyone trying to break into the Chinese market is to think of it not as one big market but as many smaller markets.

For example, Shanghai is a significant market unto itself. The Shanghai urban area has eighteen million people in it, which makes it similar in size to Chile or the Netherlands. Shanghai is also relatively easy to get in and out of and has resources available for American companies, including consultants and tradespeople who will work with you.

Whether it's Shanghai, Beijing, or somewhere else, pick a city as a market. If you do well there, you can expand into other places in China.

Another factor to consider is the relationship between Taiwan and China. We tend to focus on them as divided political entities, and yet, on an operational level, they are not nearly as split as we tend to think. There are still a lot of family and commercial connections between Taiwan and China, and from China's point of view, Taiwan is a Chinese province. This makes it possible to establish a base in Taiwan before moving into the Chinese market. One advantage of Taiwan is that for several decades longer than the mainland they've had a developed, Western-style economy that will feel more familiar to Americans. You're more likely to find people there who speak English and share your approach to doing business.

Yet you'll also be in a place with a cultural affinity for China and deep connections to the market there, which will help you transition into mainland China. You may even consider using a Taiwanese person as your market representative in China. This is quite common; whole communities of expats in China are made up of Taiwanese who are leading operations for Western companies entering the Chinese market.

THE EUROPEAN UNION: ONE MARKET OR MANY?

Now that we've examined the "hottest" international market, let's look at the second largest world market behind the United States—the EU. Before we look at individual markets, it's important to define a few terms for this region that commonly get confused. For example, the EU is a political and economic union of twenty-eight member states. The Eurozone, on the other hand, refers to the nineteen countries that use the euro as their common currency. Notably not using the euro are the United Kingdom, Denmark, and Sweden. There are also some non-EU countries that do use the euro, including Monaco and Andorra.

Knowing if a particular country is a member of the EU, Eurozone, or both is important because it will play a role in areas such as pricing. Of course, even Eurozone countries, which share the same currency, don't necessarily have the same fiscal policy. This can mean different economic results. Part of the reason Greece is a very different market than fellow Eurozone country Germany is because of the differences in their fiscal policy.

Another term that often gets confused with these is the Schengen Area, which is a zone in Europe where people can travel across borders without a passport. However, not every EU country is in the Schengen Area. You'll need to be aware if you're operating in Schengen countries or not, as this will impact how easily you can move things across borders and determine how much connected areas seem like one market.

Now that you understand what the EU is and isn't, the next question to consider is whether the EU should be viewed as one market or several small markets.

The answer is both.

Let's look first at the ways the EU feels like one market, starting with the highly integrated, well-developed transportation infrastructure that connects its countries. If you're using freight trains or trucks to transport your product or deliver your services, it's very easy to get around and across borders (especially in the Schengen Area).

EU countries also share a transnational regulatory framework. In the United States, there are state regulations but also a federal regulatory authority. Similarly, the EU has regulatory requirements concerning things such as consumer protection and antitrust compliance that every nation must abide. If you meet those requirements in one EU country, you will be in good standing in other markets or countries in the EU.

Regulations also remind us that the EU consists of multiple markets. Just as every state in the United States may have environmental, workplace, or labor regulations that are different and in some ways more restrictive than the federal regulations, the same is true for the EU. Your business may be compliant with the EU's regulations, but there may still be additional regulatory requirements in any given member country.

Another way EU countries differ is, of course, the different languages spoken in many of them. Different languages mean having to translate printed material and advertisements, plus needing multilingual salespeople if you serve customers in different countries.

The unemployment rates in the various EU countries also differ, ranging from a normalized full employment rate in Germany, to a rate in France that hovers around 10 percent. This can have an impact, for example, if you're looking to hire a local sales rep.

But perhaps the most substantial way the EU feels like many markets is that the political union has not eliminated local cultural affinities. The French are still the French, and the Polish are still the Polish, and they have different worldviews that you must consider when you're looking for a match with your value proposition.

Finally, how you view the EU depends on the type of product you sell. If you operate at the global level, the EU probably looks like a single market. You'll be selling a good that's made to a global standard, its pricing is based principally on global competition, and you can use the Eurozone and the integrated transportation infrastructure to move things around. But if you're like most small- and medium-sized businesses and you operate at the glocal or local levels, the EU will look like multiple markets and needs to be addressed as such.

When you talk about doing business in Europe, one topic that inevitably comes up is the effect of the recent debt crisis. The truth is that this "crisis" is not as widespread as we think. It's more of a localized phenomenon that reminds us that EU countries can vary enormously. The debt crisis looks very different from the creditor side in Germany than it does from the debtor side in countries like Greece and Portugal. These differences are the result of the common monetary policy for EU countries but their individual fiscal policies.

One way the debt crisis could impact companies looking to expand to the EU is financing. You may deal with customers who are dependent on inventory financing in order to buy your product, or who are sensitive to other kinds of business financing for their own operations. How challenging this issue is will depend on the country.

The debt crisis's greatest threat to potential exporters remains, for now at least, just a possibility. A country could decide to break away from the Eurozone and devalue its currency to make their products more competitive for export elsewhere in Europe. Were the EU countries in fact independent market economies with distinct currencies and banking systems, that is probably what a country like Greece would do.

If this were to happen with any EU country, it would make foreign goods less competitive on an export basis going into that market. Established companies in this market could easily lose their investment overnight. That is why, even if a company is looking at the EU as one market, I'd suggest focusing initially on more stable places such as Germany, France, Ireland, or the Scandinavian countries and growing from there.

If breaking into the European market feels overwhelming, you can approach it like China and start with a smaller market, then expand from there if you're successful.

Before Brexit—the UK's vote to depart the EU in 2016— the UK was considered by many companies to be the best initial European market for American companies. Make no mistake, the UK is still an excellent choice and companies wouldn't be wrong to start there. You don't have to worry about a language barrier in terms of your company's literature or doing business with people on the ground. It's one of the top five or six markets in the world currently, and some would even argue that it will be a more successful market after leaving the EU.

If I were looking to bring an American company to a market in the EU, I'd look first at the Republic of Ireland. Like the UK, English is the national language there, and the Irish have a strong cultural affinity with Americans. Unlike the UK, Ireland is part of the Eurozone and uses the euro, which gives you a leg up with pricing, accounting, and currency fluctuation. It also gives you a head start on entering other markets in the EU. On that same note, because you're operating in an EU member country, if you get registrations and regulatory requirements cleared in Ireland, you can go to other EU countries without issue.

Ireland has another surprising advantage over the UK—the worldview of the Irish people is more attuned to the worldview of the continent. Whereas the UK voted to leave the EU, that's a decision I don't think the Irish people would ever make. In fact, I think the Irish people would vote overwhelmingly to stay in the EU.

I think this is partially because Ireland, as a small island country, has depended on trading with other countries. This is a country with a long history of cultural integration in that sense. Over the centuries, ideas and attitudes between the Irish people and their neighbors across the European continent have become linked, leading to a stronger cultural affinity with the continent than what you'd find in the UK.

JAPAN: TECHNOLOGICAL AFFINITY AND A WORTHWHILE CHALLENGE

After the EU and China, Japan is the next largest market in the world in terms of GDP. As a market, it has many attractive qualities, starting with its population of roughly 130 million people who share a common currency, language, and cultural orientation. When you add in their sophisticated transportation infrastructure and the strong economic relations with the United States dating back to the end of World War II, the case for Japan seems even stronger.

But Japan poses challenges not found in markets such as the EU. One that we've mentioned already is the orientation toward a group identity rather than an individual identity. This preference manifests in a couple of ways, the first of which you'll notice when you interact with a group of Japanese businesspeople.

I was in Tokyo once working on a construction project with one of the leading companies in the area. As American businesspeople often do, I asked three of the men I was working with how much of their business came from one particular area. In the United States, you'd get a response such as, "Sixty-five percent of our business comes from that area." You might get a more accurate number if you pressed, but whoever answers usually provides a confident response.

The three men conferred in Japanese for a moment, then told me, "Between 30 and 70 percent" of their business was in the area I asked about. As Americans, we likely wouldn't answer this way because it's such a vague response. But in this instance, there was likely a wide range of answers among the three men, and they didn't want anyone to feel offended or disrespected by the answer that was given. It's a strange juxtaposition—the individual is respected in regard to the consensus, but individual input by itself is not as valued.

The second way this group identity plays out poses a larger challenge in the context of business. While I've found that the Japanese are some of the warmest, most wonderful people on Earth, I've never been treated as part of their group. They are amazing hosts, but no matter how hard you try to fit in, you will remain a feted, well-respected guest. You will never be a part of the club, which makes Japan a tough market to break into.

Another issue is that there is a relatively high degree of secondary protectionism around the Japanese market. The government has a particular way of interacting with businesses and has implemented a number of economic restrictions.

Still, it is possible to break into the Japanese market, and if you succeed, the rewards are well worth the effort.

The relationship between the Japanese people and the products they purchase reminds me a lot of Americans, especially when it comes to technology. Unlike China, where tech companies have their apps or websites blocked, Japan and its people have fully embraced the digital age and welcome companies of this ilk. Furthermore, the Japanese market is as loyal as any you'll find. Once you've established the right connections, it offers a sustainable position, because those connections will remain loyal to you.

NAFTA: DIVERSE OPPORTUNITIES IN MEXICO AND CANADA

The majority of the lessons in this book and the strategic thinking behind them apply regardless of the country that is your home market. They apply even if you are based in a country looking to the United States as a possible new foreign export market. But as a businessperson, consultant, and teacher who is an American based in the United States, I would be remiss if I didn't spend a few minutes addressing the two international markets closest to home for the businesses that will likely be the largest audience for this book—namely, our immediate neighbors Mexico and Canada.

As you know from the very first page of the book, my own international business experience began in Mexico. The market in Mexico has grown and matured in important ways over the past several decades. What was once a country with a highly bifurcated classist economy with the vast majority of its wealth concentrated in the hands of a very few has become a country with a vibrant middle and management class with a much greater stake in economic and political outcomes.

In this respect, Mexico resembles China. The two markets are also similar in the relative importance of the cost of labor versus the cost of goods in driving business purchasing and investment decisions. Unlike a market such as the United States, in Mexico, as in China, labor is cheap compared to highly integrated goods so that investment decisions will favor solutions that require more labor and less materials. The similar growth paths are also reflected in the most recent per capita GDP data from the International Monetary Fund (IMF). You'll find Mexico ranked seventieth with a per capita GDP of $9,249 just ahead of China ranked seventy-third with a per capita GDP of $8,583.

I sometimes recommend to businesses in the United States that if their initial evaluation of markets leads them to believe that China would be a good candidate for their business, but the distance, time zone, language, and cultural challenges presented by China seem overwhelming, they should take a closer look at Mexico as a possible market. Mexico is a large and diverse country, and at its heart is Mexico City, which is the largest metropolitan area in North America and second only to São Paolo among the largest cities in all of the Americas.

Unlike China, of course, Mexico is a much shorter flight, and doing business there requires very little time zone adjustment. Goods can be shipped entirely by land. On most products, you get all the advantages of being a part of the North American Free Trade Agreement (NAFTA).

You also get to cut your teeth on many of the challenges of exporting, such as dealing with language differences, doing business in a different currency, and practicing your ability to adapt to a different cultural context. In this case, it is a culture replete with delicious food, lively music, a rich history, and warm and welcoming people. If you are successful in Mexico, it then also provides a great base for future opportunities focused farther south in Latin America.

If instead of a market like Mexico or China, you think your business is a better fit in a market in Northern Europe where, among other things, the relationship between the cost of goods and the cost of labor more closely resemble that in the United States, but you're not quite ready to cross the ocean, then Canada might be a very attractive market to look at. As with the United States, Canada is ranked in the top twenty in per capita income.

While it may not feel entirely like it if you have traveled through much of Canada, this is very much an export play. You will have to master all of the same issues around export documentation and compliance, a different currency, and because of Canada's bilingual culture with both English and French, language and cultural differences as well.

As is the case with Mexico, however, the strain of doing business in Canada is much less than many other foreign markets. You will have shorter flights, very little time zone adjustments, and shipments of goods by land. And, again, you get all the advantages of being a part of NAFTA. There is a reason that Canada is the United States' second largest international trading partner, just behind China.

Now that we've been through an overview of the major markets, you might be ready to look closer at one market in particular. What's the next step once you're ready to move forward? Well, the research is just beginning. You need to further study the specifics of your market using the wealth of resources available to every business. After that, it's time to get on the ground in your potential market so you can begin to understand it on a deeper level. Only then can you truly determine if it's worth taking your business there.

One of the best ways I've found to conduct on-the-ground

research in your new market is by attending trade shows there. Let's jump into the next chapter and explore the benefits of attending these shows and lay out one big mistake your business must avoid.

CHAPTER 4

DUE DILIGENCE ON THE GROUND: THERE'S NO SUBSTITUTE

As we know, when you want to take your business international, it's not enough to pick a promising market and try your luck. Once you've identified a market where you believe your value proposition will resonate, the next step is familiarizing yourself with every aspect of it—the culture, geography, economy, government, competitors, risks, rewards, and more. Proactive market selection involves being proactive in every phase of this process. Knowledge is the currency you need to make this international investment.

So how do you acquire the knowledge you need? We've discussed some of the larger markets, but a view from ten thousand feet is not comprehensive enough. You will need to get on the ground. I will explain in a moment why trade shows offer crucial on-the-ground insight. But before attending a trade show, you need to conduct more research so you know where to go.

I'm not talking about browsing Google results for your market and gleaning "intel" from websites like Wikipedia. You need actionable, verified data that can help you make decisions. Thankfully, there are some amazing resources available to businesses.

THE BEST RESOURCES FOR EASY AND AFFORDABLE MARKET RESEARCH

The Central Intelligence Agency (CIA) gathers intelligence around the world for the United States and publishes its findings in the CIA *World Factbook*, which is available online. There is a report for every country that features essential background information, including data on the country's economy, demographics, and any political concerns.

It'll give you a feel for how heavily certain industries are regulated and how much the government protects its economy against foreign companies. You'll also get a sense of risk probability and issues you might encounter while breaking into a specific market.

Another great site is globalEDGE. This is a tremendous, easy-to-navigate web resource compiled and updated by the International Business Center at Michigan State University. There's a section you have to pay to use, but the free area has a plethora of economic statistics. You'll find key economic data such as a country's leading imports and exports and if they're part of a free trade agreement.

I've mentioned these organizations already, but I want to reiterate here how useful government-sponsored trade promotion offices and the experts they employ can be to your business. There are dozens of USEAC offices across the United States that exist to help American businesses succeed internationally.

The US Department of State has embassies and consulates around the world, and in each of these locations you'll find a branch of the Department of Commerce with staff reporting to a senior commercial officer. Additionally, most states have an office of the Department of Commerce that can provide access to the department's vast global trade network.

Every state and many large US cities also have someone in their economic development office whose role is to help local businesses succeed internationally. If you are not a US business, you may find that your country's economic development office offers similar services. If you don't know where to begin navigating all of these resources, your local World Trade Center can help steer you in the right direction.

Depending on your company's resources and how committed you are to international expansion, it might be worth hiring a private market specialist. Some specialize in a particular industry and can help you navigate markets within those sectors. Others focus on specific regions or countries. They can help you understand market factors that may not show up on a report—cultural nuances or political red flags, for example. If they're really worth the money, they'll also help you make connections with the right kinds of people.

Take a moment to look at the list of references and resources following the conclusion of this book. You will find the resources mentioned here as well as other websites, books, and organizations that can prove invaluable in acquiring the necessary market data.

TRADE SHOWS—GO BEFORE YOU GO GLOCAL

These are just a few resources that can help you build a foundation of knowledge. Once you've zeroed in on a market, it's time to get on the ground so you begin meeting people and soaking up every aspect of the culture and business environment there. Journeying to a foreign country where the people might speak a different language can feel daunting, but trade shows provide an efficient method of researching and interacting with people all in one place.

The biggest mistake I see businesses make when it comes to trade shows is attending them to promote their product or service only *after* they've broken into the market. This backward approach deprives them of the best opportunity they have for research ahead of entering a new market. Trade shows aren't just for promotion; they can help your business simply because they're an incredibly useful and rich source of market intel.

The appeal of trade shows is that they shrink your market down to a single location. Rather than wandering around your market's capital city hoping to find distributors, identify competitors, or better understand the culture, you can experience a concentrated version of that market where many of the companies and individuals you'll need to know about are all together.

Every major industry has a trade show at least once a year in almost every major market in the world. A simple Google search will reveal most of the shows worth attending, and if you need further assistance, you can contact some of the local experts we mentioned earlier. Once you've identified the top show for your industry in your market, sign up and go!

Before you depart, buy a few travel guides for the country you're visiting. In addition to restaurant and hotel recommendations, the good ones always have front sections on political history, cultural practices, and some keys to basic cultural orientation. Even if it's on your flight to your destination, read these before you arrive.

Once you're there, you'll see what products are being offered in this market. You'll learn what the supply chain looks like, because front-end retailers and back-end suppliers, support products, and software designers attend. The competitive environment will start to come into focus as you see the companies that attend and, judging by the size of their booths, get an idea of the big players. You might discover huge companies that have zero presence in your home market, plus a host of local companies worth knowing about.

Keep in mind that not all your competitors will be present in the most conventional way, with a booth, but they'll be there in some capacity. They may be walking around or giving a presentation. When you sign up for the show, you'll receive a list of vendors and presenters you should consider following up with when you get home.

Trade shows are also a great resource for pricing information. Visit the booths and act like an interested customer. The reps will happily give you brochures, pricing information, and other insightful resources that might not be available anywhere else.

Finally, trade shows can help you understand the technology in your market. You'll see what cutting-edge products are being offered, where the market is headed, and what technology is required to be part of it. As I've learned firsthand and will discuss in the next section, what you learn about technology can be especially eye-opening.

One final tip for making the most of your trade show experience is to pull out the phone book in your hotel room. Hotels in most countries keep some version of a Yellow Pages in rooms. Find your product or industry, then look for prominent names or logos. You may find distributors, retailers, or competitors that weren't at the show.

I've experienced the advantages of trade shows firsthand. I worked in the building industry for much of my career and would attend what is now called the Dach und Holz (Roof and Wood), an annual trade show in Germany focused on building products in the European market. All in one place, I was able to see who the players were, evaluate the different companies, and learn about competitors who didn't have a presence in the United States.

I gained some surprising insights. For example, I realized that in many areas of the building industry, the United

States is at least three to five years behind Europe, possibly due to how litigious the US market has become. I would routinely see new products at the Dach und Holz that wouldn't get to the United States for five years, and when they did, they'd be the hot new thing.

Once I saw that Europe was several years ahead of the United States on the technology curve, I had to reconsider whether our American company could be successful there. The flip side of this sobering realization was that I got a glimpse of the future while at the Dach und Holz and saw what was coming down the road in my domestic market. Additionally, I discovered companies that didn't participate in the US market, yet were significant players in Europe and other global markets such as South America. This intelligence was useful if my company started looking to break into other international markets.

You may come away from a trade show with unexpected knowledge about how your current product might perform, or how another product you've created may be more valuable. That's what happened to me the first year I attended the Expo CIHAC, Mexico's major building industry trade show.

I discovered that although large industrial roofing installations in the United States rely on corrugated steel roof decking, in Mexico, as well as many other countries in the world, commercial construction is done principally with structural concrete. Unlike corrugated steel, concrete roofs don't need separate insulation. There is a very limited market in Mexico for a product that is the industry standard in the United States. On the other hand, waterproofing the concrete was a major focus, and it turned out there was an opening for American-made plasticized coatings.

I had gone to the Expo CIHAC thinking that we had top-of-the-line, cutting-edge products the world needed and wanted, and found out we would be only a minor niche player in the Mexican market, because it's not the technology that people there required. On the other hand, I was able to understand the opportunities there for other products better suited to the market. These are things I probably wouldn't have learned by doing web research, but on the ground, this insight became abundantly clear.

The ability to gain insight into your new market and gauge how your product would be received there is only one perk of attending trade shows. The other huge benefit is the opportunity to meet people and network with others in your industry, some of whom might become valuable partners in your international endeavors. I saw this happen for a small company that was looking to take their tabletop gaming business to China. I told them to find a trade show there, and after some research, we discovered the Game

Developers Conference in Shanghai and they signed up to attend.

At the show, they learned about the Chinese culture and how certain gaming characters would be interpreted differently than they would in the United States. For example, many American fantasy games involving a quest might have the characters run into scary, fire-breathing dragons that must be slain. But in China, dragons are revered creatures. So instead of having them as enemies, the magical beasts should be allies for characters in the game.

Cultural nuances like this continued to come up during their time at the show, including the fact that in Shanghai, tabletop gaming tends to take place at special cafés as opposed to playing at home with your group of friends. At the trade show, my client met the owner of one of these gaming cafés who agreed to stock and sponsor his game, thus becoming his initial outlet for expansion into China.

The trade show experience isn't just for finding better opportunities on the sales end; you may also be able to make relationships that open doors on the front end of the supply chain. After making some design changes to better adapt the game to the Chinese culture, my client is now working with a manufacturing company he connected with at the conference. This manufacturer might become the principal supplier of boards, cards, and pieces for their games in the United States.

Simply by attending a trade show in their potential market and networking with the people there, my client found a café owner willing to sponsor and stock their game, plus a new supplier for China and possibly the United States. These valuable connections, plus the insights you can gain into the market and the culture, make trade shows a crucial step in the research process, as you can consider whether to enter an international market.

Trade shows condense your market into a central location for a short period. All the major players and hottest products will be there, which means you should be, too. As you prepare to go, keep the following questions in mind so you get the most out of your experience:

- What is the scope of the market specifically for your product?
- How do customers address the problems that your product seeks to address?
- Who are your competitors?
- Who are potential distributors and retail outlets?
- Which manufacturers could you plug into the front end of your supply chain?
- Will you be a mainstream, major market player or a niche market player?

✿ Does your product need a redesign for this market?

Once you've identified a fit with your value proposition, done the initial research, and gathered on-the-ground knowledge from a trade show, you can make an informed decision of whether your potential market is worth pursuing. If it is, the next step is preparing to address the challenges your business will face during this process. That's what we'll cover in the next two chapters, starting with some major operational issues.

MARKET READINESS: ALIGNING YOUR ORGANIZATIONAL CULTURE FOR SUCCESS

CHAPTER 5

EXPORT READINESS: OPERATIONS, SALES, MARKETING, AND CUSTOMER SERVICE

The number one mistake businesses make when expanding internationally isn't doing the wrong thing but going to the wrong market. The second biggest mistake is failing to get their company export-ready across every department—operations, sales, marketing, and customer service. To be successful in a new market, some things will have to change, and these changes create a ripple effect that can result in challenges elsewhere.

There will be issues that arise as you prepare to go international. The key is to be aware of potential challenges, so you can work to solve them before they pop up, not after. That's an idea you'll see repeated throughout this chapter—preparation. As Benjamin Franklin put it, "By failing to prepare, you are preparing to fail." Before you ever ship the first product or provide service to the first customer, there are questions you'll need to answer.

We know that a one-size-fits-all approach doesn't work when you begin serving customers in a new market, yet many companies make this mistake. They plow ahead thinking that international customers will respond to their product or service in the same way their domestic customers do. Doing business internationally means adapting what you do to fit the demands of your new market. If you produce a physical product, those changes will usually begin with manufacturing.

MAKING WHAT YOUR CUSTOMERS WANT AND NEED

If you're moving a product into a new market, you'll likely have to make changes so the product is appealing to local consumers. To start with, the basic appearance of your product may have to be modified. This could mean a change in color, or if it's a food product, a taste or texture aspect that you need to alter.

If homes and offices in your new market are smaller than

in your domestic market, the size of your product may also need to change. If this happens, you'll need to consider if the equipment at your manufacturing plant can produce products with new dimensions.

If your product runs on electricity, the plug on the end of the cord will need to change, because countries have different socket shapes. A transformer may need to be built in so your product can function on another country's electrical grid.

Packaging is another area where you'll probably have to make adjustments. Because you'll be shipping your product longer distances in different types of conveyances and in potentially challenging weather, your product's packaging must be able to hold up for the duration of the shipping process. The last thing you want is a shipment of your product arriving damaged to a new customer because the packaging fell apart.

Closely related to packaging is labeling, which will obviously need to change if customers in your new market speak a different language. There may also be regulations requiring certain disclosures. In fact, compliance is one thing you'll have to pay close attention to when you're getting your product ready for this new market. Be sure you understand local requirements regarding fire and safety codes and consumer disclosure information codes, among others. We'll cover more compliance issues and international regulations for you to consider in the next chapter. Once you're certain of the guidelines your product must follow, and what information needs to be included on labels, you'll be better able to determine their impact on manufacturing.

Each of these design changes comes with a variety of challenges. But often, the most difficult modification is one that may not have occurred to you yet, which is measurements.

For products that have specific dimensions, if you've been strictly doing business in the United States, your company has probably been making these to an imperial measure— pounds and ounces, feet and inches. When you go abroad, however, you learn quickly that we're one of three countries in the world that doesn't use the metric system.

This will be an issue for you in several respects. Many small- and medium-sized companies simply do conversions when they quote or sell their products, rather than modifying the products. Instead of price per pound, for example, they quote the price per kilogram. This can work on a small scale, but the more complex things get, the more opportunities there are for the conversion factor to get screwed up somewhere.

If someone accidentally flips the numerator and denominator when trying to give a quote, your company could wind up overcharging, which means you'll likely never get repeat business from that client—or undercharging, which means you've just committed to a sale where you're going to lose your shirt.

One solution to the conversion problem is to change specifications for the overseas market, so that those products are made and sold in metric sizes and weights. The issue with this strategy, obviously, is you have to keep changing your manufacturing process and adding new layers of inventory to packaging and product.

A long-term solution is to transition from a strictly domestic company to an international one and change your entire process to reflect that commitment. In this scenario, even the products for your domestic market are made in metric measures. The drawback here is the cost and finality of such a commitment and its impact on domestic customers whose operations are configured to imperial measures.

Measurement issues not only affect your product as manufactured but also compatibility with systems down the line. For example, if you make machinery and decide to keep making your product to its current imperial specifications as you go international, you'll find that the materials you use to put your product together—the literal nuts and bolts—can create problems for your new customers.

If your product's screws, nuts, and bolts are threaded in imperial sizes, but the spare parts necessary for simple maintenance repairs sourced by your customer are metrically threaded, they won't fit your product, and you've created a serious maintenance problem for your customer. One solution for this issue would be have separate packages of hardware that you can ship along with the product, but this adds a new layer of complexity and cost as well.

Ultimately, you'll have to examine how measurement differences affect your manufacturing line. Is your plant equipped to handle making products to new dimensions using new measurements? If not, you'll have to carefully train your sales and support teams to reliably and consistently make the necessary conversions. If it is, what happens when you change the manufacturing process for the overseas version of your product? How does that affect the shutdown and restart times of your production line? Who will be responsible for designing and executing this modified version of your product? Communication is critical in preparing for a new market, not only in terms of considering these questions with leadership but also keeping those team members who will be doing the work in the loop on what's being decided.

MANAGING YOUR EXPANDING INVENTORY

One of the biggest challenges every company faces and

seeks to manage is keeping its working capital down. A big part of this challenge is limiting the amount of money tied up in raw materials waiting to be used in the production process, as well as finished product that's come off the line but is waiting to be shipped, sold, and paid for by the customer.

Expanding into a new market makes this issue more difficult to manage. If you're sourcing new raw materials to make modified products for overseas markets, now you have more raw material than before. If you have products coming off the line in different shapes and sizes, and with different attachments, labeling, and packaging, obviously you've greatly added to your inventory. This may mean you've also added SKUs, which puts another burden on the people in the operations and warehouse end of your business.

As you increase your inventory, keeping everything straight becomes more complex. Making sure that stock is organized and accessible so the correct product is put in the correct container bound for the correct customer seems straightforward, but I know many companies struggle in this area initially when going international. Somehow, their product winds up getting on a container bound for another market, and next thing they know, they have a container loaded with the wrong products sitting in a port with a customer who refuses to accept it because it's not what they ordered.

Mistakes will happen, but the key to stopping them from happening consistently and crippling your international efforts is preparation. Have the conversation with your warehouse and operations staff well before new inventory is added.

Closely tied to the issue of inventory management is shipping, which also gets more complex once you begin exporting products overseas. As previously mentioned, the modes of transportation change. When you sell products domestically, they're probably put on a truck and sent down the highway. When you're selling internationally, most items will be shipped in intermodal ocean freight containers if there's a high enough volume.

Containerization, or how these containers get loaded, works a lot like packing the back end of a semitrailer. But instead of spending a couple of days on a highway, your product spends four to six weeks on a container ship in the middle of the ocean. During this transit, the temperature can fluctuate from over 100 degrees to below freezing.

The final leg of the shipment is also far different. You may have adapted your packaging for an ocean freight container, but when that container arrives at the receiving port and your goods get unloaded to begin transport to your customer, things get tricky.

The trucks being used may be different dimensions than those used in your domestic market or than the containers themselves. If you've designed your packaging to fit two pallets wide and two pallets high in an ocean freight container, it now must get to your final customer in a vehicle that looks far different. Truck drivers can be very creative when it comes to making your package fit on their truck, but that likely means deconstructing your packaging to make things work.

Additional due diligence is required to make sure the final leg of your shipping process doesn't leave the customer with a package that in no way resembles what you sent them. Know the dimensions of every vehicle that will be used to transport your product and adapt your packaging so it doesn't get dismantled by a creative truck driver.

A longer shipping process means more risk, so you'll have to decide how to handle that risk with your buyer. If I'm a seller, in theory I would rather transfer title and risk to my buyer as soon as possible. Conversely, if I'm a buyer, I would want, again in theory, to take title and assume the risk as late as possible in the process. But it isn't that simple.

For example, while a seller may legally transfer title and the risk of loss to a buyer early in the process, if the buyer receives goods that are defective or nonconforming in some way, either due to damage that occurred during shipment or another reason, it's still a customer service problem for the seller. Regardless of the legal implications, the seller must still resolve this problem if they want a happy, ongoing relationship with the customer.

By giving up the shipping risk, a seller also gives up a measure of control. They don't get to choose things such as the shipping method or carrier, so if the goods arrive in less-than-ideal condition, they can only wonder what would've happened had they maintained control.

EXTENDING CREDIT AND GETTING PAID

If you're selling internationally, your sales cycle will be longer. One major reason is that transporting goods overseas via cargo ships increases the shipping time frame from a few days to as much as a couple of months. As a result, the time between when your product is manufactured and when your customer receives it can be up to ten times longer.

A longer sales cycle will affect your company's financial performance, particularly if you extend credit terms. Companies starting out in the international market with a small product might be able to get cash in advance or have customers pay with a credit card.

But if you're selling on a large scale, a single container

of your product could be worth hundreds of thousands of dollars. That's too much at stake for a customer to be willing to pay cash in advance. As a temporary solution, some businesses use what is known as a letter of credit to get paid. This document provides you with some security, as there is an intermediate bank that guarantees the payment to your company assuming the shipment conforms to what was agreed upon in the purchase contract.

Letters of credit can be tricky, though, because several things can happen during an international shipment (e.g., a change in the vessel) that can cause some aspect of the export documentation—the invoice or the bill of lading, for example—to be nonconforming with the letter of credit. If that happens, it will negate the bank's liability to be a guarantor and leave you waiting for payment from the customer after having shipped the goods.

The other problem with letters of credit is that most customers can't get one without posting security on the front end that's nearly equal to the amount owed. So the customer may not be paying $100,000 in advance, but they're nonetheless tying up the equivalent in cash or capital for a couple of months while the product is shipped to them. For some customers that may be asking too much to facilitate a sale, especially if there's local competition.

You'll need to find a credit solution that works for your

business and your customers if you're seeking large-scale, long-term success. Keep in mind that in the United States, most customers use credit to make purchases; your international customers will likely do the same. Local competitors are a threat in this area, because they can offer credit terms you may not be able to match because they're not dealing with the costs or delays of shipping products overseas.

If you do extend credit terms, you'll need to verify the credit worthiness of your foreign customers. There are foreign agencies that work much like Dun & Bradstreet in the United States that can help with this process, as can the US Department of Commerce.

After receiving your product, some customers may wait until after they sell the product to pay the invoice they have with your company. In other words, your sales cycle is impacted by their sales cycle. What you may end up realizing is that for your credit terms to work in facilitating sales, you'll be dealing with a period of 90–120 days, or sometimes even longer.

If you're paying supplier invoices within thirty or forty-five days, but your customers aren't paying for 90 or 120 days, you're essentially loaning those customers a lot of money, interest-free, for an extended period. This disparity can have serious consequences for cash flow and the ultimate success of your business, so it's important to manage it effectively.

The difference between domestic credit terms and international terms can create friction within your organization. If the accounting department is being told to push for thirty-day terms and the international rep is offering 120-day terms, your accounting staff might be upset, because they're the ones dealing with the challenges this disparity creates. This is a functional issue that must be addressed, but it's also a cultural one. In the next chapter, we'll look at how to deal with the effect international sales has on your company culture.

Even if you don't extend credit terms, you should prepare for the impact of foreign currency. If you keep your prices in US dollars, there is an exchange risk to the buyer. If the value of the dollar fluctuates between the time they place their order and the time they pay it, one party will end up less well-off. If the buyer ends up paying more, they may choose to buy from a local competitor in the future to avoid this issue.

There is also a risk in some markets of a significant devaluation of the local currency. For example, if the country experiences a financial crisis and devalues its currency to the point that your goods are no longer competitively priced, you can lose your market position overnight.

There are no easy answers when it comes to getting paid for international sales, but planning in advance beats learning hard lessons after the fact. Choose the solutions that work best for your company and prepare for the implications of those choices. The best strategy is to do the due diligence on your new customers.

MARKETING IN A NEW LANGUAGE

Your marketing staff has another set of challenges when doing business abroad, most notably the impact of a new language. Not only will they need to translate the company's literature—brochures, manuals, and more—into the local language, but they'll also need to translate parts of your website, or they'll have to set up a new website entirely.

When considering what to translate, keep in mind that a new set of customers may have different preferences for how they receive information. They might prefer getting information online or in the form of demonstration videos so the language barriers are less of an issue.

I've seen some companies try to cut corners when dealing with language differences. If the person they're dealing with speaks sufficient English to complete the transaction, they falsely assume that translation isn't a big concern. What they fail to realize is that if their product is being used by someone else down the line who doesn't speak English, how well can they understand what the product is or how it's supposed to work?

Even companies that understand this aren't guaranteed to be understood. Most of us don't fully appreciate the extent to which we use local idioms and expressions that don't translate well. Going the cheap route and using Google Translate for your marketing materials won't suffice when the result is incomprehensible even for a native English speaker. Invest in your success by hiring a translator from your new market. Even then, keep in mind that person may be qualified for a general translation but may not understand industry slang or other linguistic oddities peculiar to your industry.

I learned this firsthand when I got involved in international business and had some company literature translated into Spanish by a service in Denver that, as I understood it, was highly qualified. I sent the piece to my new partners in Mexico, feeling pretty good, because I thought I was ahead of the game. My people in Mexico read it, had a huge laugh over it, and then retranslated the entire thing. The document I'd sent them was correctly translated, literally, but the literal translation of the American euphemisms and idiomatic expressions used in our industry did not describe the same things in this new market. The translation was technically correct but utterly useless for the people who read it.

That situation helped me figure out a good translation technique. As you're making your foreign contacts and getting resources put together, find someone in the country who is familiar with your industry and the expressions associated with it. Have them either do your translations or vet a translation by someone else to make sure it's usable and not just a literal—but incorrect—translation of your source material.

This brings up another helpful strategy. Imagine you suddenly make a change to your product, or you realize your current company literature isn't appealing to customers. You might need to add something, make an edit, or completely change it. One of the great things about having a website that's accessible to all your markets is that you could have your company literature posted there in pdf format so it can be downloaded and printed out as needed by a distributor, sales agent, or customer. It's a lot cheaper to allow access to updated literature electronically than it is to reprint thousands of copies.

But translating a website is about more than practicality and accessibility. By having pages or even an entire version of your site in a local language, you're communicating to customers and potential partners in this new market that this is a serious venture for you. That's a good reason to consider translating at least some of your site before you even start shipping to the new market. This way, if someone you meet at a trade show looks up your company online, they'll already find information in their language.

Another way to make a good impression with your website is to give your customers access to things the public wouldn't have, such as pricing information or the ability to place orders via a special portal where they can sign in. This will make your new customers feel recognized and special, and when that happens, positive reactions about your business will be reinforced. Treat your current and potential foreign customers with consideration regarding their language, and they're likely to be very responsive.

PRICING STRATEGY: A MARKETING MUST

Getting the price right will be a critical task for your marketing team. Like any other piece of marketing, pricing is information a company uses to convey value to customers. When it comes to your new market, the marketing department needs to set the price, and your sales team should be prepared to sell its value.

The first factor that drives pricing is the company's need to make a profit, which means the price of your product must be a certain percentage above its cost. As we know, a foreign market includes more costs than a domestic one. You'll need different packaging and labeling, possible manufacturing changeovers, higher shipping costs, import duties and tariffs, compliance with new regulations, and translating marketing materials, to name a few. Because your expenses are higher, there is a certain pricing threshold you can't go below.

The other thing driving your pricing decision is, of course, competition. When you get beyond a certain price point, customers will decide to use another product. You will need to consider locally available substitutes and how their value to customers compares to the value your product offers. Study your competitors to learn what they're making and how much they're charging. Your price needs to reflect a profit-driven mindset, but it can't be made unrealistic by the presence of local competition that has much lower shipping and import costs. This will bring you back to the root question, "Does your value proposition hold up? Is it strong enough that you can sell your product's value and not its price?"

Companies that are failing overseas often lose sight of this. They assume if they sell their product for a certain price in one place, they'll sell it for roughly the same price elsewhere, and they lock themselves into that amount.

Sales reps can be part of the problem. If they don't thoroughly understand and buy into the company's value proposition, they won't be able to translate that value to customers. The refrain you'll likely hear is, "I could sell more of these if you would just lower the price."

But they've missed the point. It's not about the price; it's about the product's value.

CUSTOMER SERVICE CHALLENGES

Given the challenges elsewhere, it shouldn't be surprising that customer service will also be affected when your company expands into an overseas market. What is surprising is how these challenges pop up in areas that don't immediately come to mind.

For instance, customer service has ties to shipping and logistics. To answer questions and resolve problems, your customer service staff needs to become familiar with the many documents and certifications that different markets require for imported goods (we'll look at these in the next chapter). They must be able to handle issues such as risk of loss, title transference, payment, insurance, and which party pays import duties.

If customers receive products in a condition different from when they left the plant, that's an issue for customer service. They must be ready with explanations, which means having an excellent understanding of different kinds of packaging and how transport may alter or damage a product. They'll need to be aware that products may be disassembled to fit onto trucks that are different sizes than the ones at your point of origin.

To that end, you'll have to decide how customers contact customer service representatives. In your domestic market, having customer service reps available during regular business hours might suffice. But if you're now doing business in a place where the middle of your customer's day is the middle of your night, will you hire more people to provide ongoing customer service? Will you outsource after-hours work?

Another issue, of course, is language. Who's going to be able to help a customer calling in Spanish, German, or Thai? If you outsource for this, you'll need systems in place to ensure the people dealing with your customers are armed with the knowledge they need. They must have the right attitude to represent your company in the best possible way.

For a lot of businesses, the key customer service interaction happens by having people on the ground who can provide in-field support. You have two options for boots-on-the-ground customer service, each of which leads to its own set of problems.

The first option is to have your domestic customer service

personnel travel to the international customer. The big issues here are added expense and the increased time it takes to get to and solve a customer's problem. It costs a lot more to send a service rep to China than it does to send him to Cleveland. You also have jet lag to deal with and the added time your reps need to recover before meeting with customers. Last, you should provide service reps with cultural-sensitivity training to help them prepare for a new culture and to be most effective in their role abroad.

The second option is to hire people in the new market who can service your customers. Aside from challenges in hiring, training, and supervising, which I'll discuss more in the next chapter, you must also understand local employment laws, including what is necessary to employ someone. You should also understand the requirements for contracts, benefits, minimum wage, and termination.

Something as simple as staying in touch with overseas employees can be a challenge. You need to know if they're showing up for work, responding appropriately to problems, and communicating larger issues back to the domestic staff to be handled. For either option, customer service should work with human resources to prepare for the challenges related to travel and serving foreign customers, which we'll cover in the next chapter.

The challenges you'll face are about more than getting

your company export-ready. Taking your business international will create cultural issues that can disrupt even the strongest businesses if they're not dealt with appropriately. Luckily, you can mitigate these problems by communicating consistently across every level of your organization from day one. Let's take a closer look at how that might work within your business.

CHAPTER 6

INTERNAL READINESS: IMPACT ON COMPANY CULTURE

Expanding into an international market comes with operational challenges that force you to change what you're doing and how you're doing it. For any savvy businessperson, it should come as no surprise that you'll have to confront these challenges. Yet there's a second effect that international expansion has on your business, one that's not as easy to anticipate—challenges to your company culture. You're not just changing the what and how of your business to enter a new market; you're also changing the why.

If every member of your organization isn't on the same page going in, there will be tension that can ultimately doom your international efforts. Worse yet, the existing business can be damaged if your company culture includes infighting and contradictory goals.

The way to prevent these issues from popping up is through consistent communication about why the company is entering a new market and what it hopes to accomplish. The message should reverberate throughout the entire organization, not just in one department or among the leadership. To be successful abroad, your company needs everyone.

But to start things off, you need buy-in from the highest levels of the company.

GET MANAGEMENT ON BOARD FROM THE START

Breaking into a new market is not a project that's handled solely by an individual or small group. For one thing, they may not be tuned in or adequately connected to all the other parts of your business that will be impacted. They'll focus on breaking into the market, and it's only after the decisions begin reverberating through your company that everyone will realize those actions have created cultural dissonance.

Pursuing a new market is truly a team effort, and that effort begins with management. To get the company on board, the decision makers should not only be clued in but also have buy-in on any international expansion plans. As I'm sure is obvious now, foreign market entry is not a side project that can be pursued on a whim. As a fundamental proposition, the growth strategy for your business should be driving your entry into new markets, not the other way around.

While it might sound obvious to check with senior management before pursuing a new market, I've seen situations where a group put a lot of time and hard work into developing an opportunity only to have someone at the top shut it down when the cultural disruptions began.

I've even had it happen to me. A team and I were working hard to make connections and get our product ready to launch in the Chinese market. Things seemed promising, and I sent a finished business plan upstairs. I just needed a final sign-off and permission to draw the check, but a few days went by, and I didn't hear anything.

Finally, I got in touch with the CEO. "You know," he admitted, "the plan looks interesting, but I didn't sign off on it because I don't want to divert resources by having you work on this China initiative instead of the other, more important things you're also focused on."

It was a perfectly legitimate decision. Still, it would

have been helpful to me if I had understood the level of ambivalence before I had already devoted so much to the new project.

Once senior management or ownership has bought in, input should be solicited from team members in manufacturing, marketing, customer service, accounting, legal, and human resources. Everyone should know up front what the goal is and what it will take to get there. Share how this new venture will impact each department, ask what challenges they expect, and figure out how to ameliorate those challenges.

This way, when you start to increase inventory and extend credit terms, the people in the departments impacted by those decisions will know what's coming and why it's happening. They will have a plan to deal with the changes, and everyone will be working together to make the organization more successful and profitable, instead of working against each other from their little silos with the fragments of information they have.

CHOOSE THE RIGHT LEADER FOR THE JOB

Getting off to a good start with international expansion also comes down to choosing the right project leader (or leaders, if a team is the better approach). The first quality a leader should have is the ability to resolve conflict among competing silos. The effort to expand into new international markets will cause disruption within the company and the ripple effect of those efforts can create competing views as to how resources are being allocated and decisions are being made.

One way to find someone skilled at conflict resolution is to look at people who have relationships with employees in multiple departments within the company. This could be the case for someone who's served in several positions, or it could be a person whose job has a widespread reach within the company. If you can't find someone who fits this profile, you should at least look for someone who takes an organization-wide view of success. That way, they'll be sensitive in working with people from every part of the organization.

I've learned about this need for communication and connection with different departments from personal experience. In fact, this is one of the areas in this book where my knowledge comes not from my success but from my failure. Fairly early in my career, I had the credit manager of our company come into my office with his hair on fire, wanting to know why I had just agreed to a distribution deal that had 120-day terms. If I'd been thinking further ahead and discussed it with him beforehand, this wouldn't have been an issue. Fortunately, we talked it through and made it work, but it took some begging, genuine understanding, and empathy to make sure I could repair that relationship.

When it comes to choosing someone to lead this effort, you must consider the impact these new duties will have on their current responsibilities. Can they balance their current workload with this new project? If they could be totally focused on international expansion, they would likely foresee more issues before they become problems. For example, a full-time person in this role could set aside time to visit the manufacturing plant and work out any issues there. But if they're trying to fit this into the few hours a day they've got for this project, those are the kinds of niceties that fall by the wayside.

Given this concern, a logical choice might be to create a new position or hire an outside consultant to lead this effort. For larger companies, this strategy is the best option. But the reality for most small- and medium-sized businesses is that it's not always realistic to add a salary and any related overhead in advance of the revenue that's supposed to support it.

The best option, then, is to find the right employee or team for this effort and give them the training and time needed to do the job right. They'll need buy-in from management, a coordinated effort across departments, and access to resources such as the USEAC and the World Trade Center to ensure they're moving in the right direction.

DON'T TAKE REGULATORY COMPLIANCE FOR GRANTED

In the last chapter, we mainly focused on preparations for the revenue-generating areas of a business, but entering a new market is about more than addressing financial concerns.

We live in a world of opportunity but also one with various legal constraints. Your legal department or outside legal resource can help you deal with unfamiliar regulations in your new market. They will help ensure that as your team pursues opportunities in this new market that you're not going to expose the company to extreme risks.

Export compliance is a major area where legal can help. Companies face various kinds of regulatory compliance, whether it's product labeling, occupational health and safety requirements, consumer disclosure and notification issues, or licensing and registration questions. Every new market you enter presents a new set of these kinds of regulatory challenges.

In addition, when you start selling products outside of your domestic market, there's a whole overlay of regulations that must be followed when exporting these products. For an American company, the first part of these are US export restrictions, which essentially fall into three main categories:

1. **Products you are not allowed to export or can export only under limited circumstances.** These generally tend to be products related to national defense and security, but there are some products that don't seem, at first glance, to belong in this category. For example, a mechanism to start an electronic home appliance might be restricted because it could be used in a missile trigger mechanism. This is sometimes referred to as the end-use problem.

2. **Restricted destinations.** For various reasons, there are countries that you cannot export to or to which you cannot export certain things. One of the biggest problems I see regarding this restriction occurs when a company acquires a foreign business with historic ties to those markets. A lot of other countries don't share our restrictions, but if an American company owns a subsidiary in another country, and that foreign subsidiary sends product to one of these prohibited destinations, the American company has just violated those regulations. I've had this come up both with a Mexican subsidiary that had sold things to Cuba and with an Italian subsidiary that had sold things to Libya. The people in those operations thought we were crazy when we ended these sales. In their minds, why wouldn't we want to sell things to Cuba or Libya?

3. **Restricted parties.** These are sanctions imposed against certain people or organizations. For example, in the current political environment, you'll some-

times encounter sanctions against certain people or businesses from Russia. If you don't have a restricted product, you can sell it in Russia. But there may still be Russian people or entities with whom you're not allowed to do business. This falls into a category called restricted party screening (RPS).

On the other side of the border, there may also be foreign import constraints. Certain products or ingredients are restricted even though it's acceptable for us to export them. For instance, Europeans have a different attitude toward genetically modified organisms (GMOs). There are significantly more regulations around them in the EU.

One of the tricky things about dealing with these import restrictions is that in my experience, regulations are frequently used as a sort of secondary trade restriction. So a country agrees through participation in the World Trade Organization or a free-trade agreement to eliminate tariffs, duties, or other constraints, but countries are generally still allowed to enforce what they perceive to be legitimate regulations for their domestic health and safety. This lets them impose regulations that restrict significant categories of products that you could otherwise sell into those markets.

Closely tied to regulatory compliance is the litany of export documentation and tracking requirements. In order to export products from the United States, you need to be savvy enough to understand our export documentation process and how to use the electronic system to enter data and the appropriate tracking numbers for your products.

The system serves many purposes. One is simply for the US government to be able to track exports of different products. This is how they're able to report statistics, exports, and trade surpluses or deficiencies in different countries. It also tracks and ensures restrictions are being followed. The importing country uses it as well to know the right schedule of applicable tariffs and duties.

This tracking system involves specific documentation. In the days of paper and ink, you needed an Export Control Declaration, but as with most data these days, this process has gone digital. Now exports are handled by the Automated Export System (AES), which submits the electronic export information (EEI). The system then produces an international transaction number (ITN) that's used to track shipments through the entire export process, from when they leave your site, to when they arrive at your customer's location.

Here are a few other documents involved in the exporting process:

✿ **Commercial Invoice and Export Packing List:** As

goods leave the United States and enter customs and import control in another country, the specificity of this invoice and the packing list are critical, because they indicate that you've complied with certain regulations and restrictions. If that isn't understood, your shipment may end up being impounded or meeting some other undesirable fate.

✿ **Bill of Lading or Air Waybill:** Like the bill of shipping, which you would fill out for a domestic trucking company, the bill of lading is included with items shipped on an ocean freight container. An air waybill is the requirement if you're shipping by air freight. These important documents describe the items being shipped and who is in control of them at certain points of the shipping process. They are essentially the key to passing title as the goods move through the shipment process.

✿ **Certificate of Origin:** This document certifies the country from which the product originated. More than a statement on your product labeling that says it is "Made in the USA," it is a certificate generated by an entity, sometimes a chamber of commerce or the World Trade Centers Association.

✿ **Certificate of Free Sale:** This document essentially states that the goods you are exporting to the new market are generally sold in open commerce in the United States. In a sense, it's a proxy indicating that your product has been recognized, tested, and performs the way customers expect. It says you're not shipping a custom-made product whose performance can't be guaranteed.

✿ **Phytosanitary Certificate:** This document often trips people up because they don't realize they need it. Most countries are concerned about importing invasive species of insects, the larvae of which frequently live in wood products. While your product itself may not be made of wood, in the United States, we predominately use wood pallets in the shipment of goods. In some countries with strict regulations on foreign wood, you won't be able to use wood pallets. In others, you'll just need the phytosanitary certificate indicating that the wood pallet has been appropriately treated.

In addition to these documents, you'll need to be familiar with terms of trade and how they differ internationally compared to domestically. For best practice, I recommend getting your terms of trade from a list of International Commercial Terms (Incoterms).

Incoterms are a proprietary set of terms codified by the International Chamber of Commerce. There are eleven terms of trade, each of which has a specific meaning related to details such as when a title transfers, who bears the risk of the loss, and who pays what costs. On one end of the seller/buyer risk allocation spectrum is:

○ Ex Works (EXW): The majority, if not all, of the risk and responsibility belongs to the buyer because they take title at the seller's location, and they assume the risk involved in getting it to them.
○ On the other end of the risk allocation spectrum is:
○ Delivered Duty Paid (DDP): The seller takes the majority, if not all, the risk and responsibility and is committing to deliver the product to the buyer with all costs paid, including any import duty.

The other terms cover points in between.

Businesspeople around the world know and use Incoterms, so it's best that your team members become familiar with and begin using them, too. You can find a basic summary of the terms online, but to fully understand the finer points and implications, you will have to purchase the Incoterms guide from the International Chamber of Commerce.

A final documentation issue to mention is that even if a free-trade agreement like NAFTA has been implemented to open market opportunities by eliminating restrictions, the agreement itself may impose certain requirements in terms of how products are handled and tracked across borders. You will need to make sure you're complying with those as well.

As these examples illustrate, there's a whole regulatory

regime related to compliance and export documentation. This is an area that requires qualified legal assistance and advice to ensure compliance. Failure to do so could result in serious penalties and lost business opportunities.

PROTECTING YOUR INTELLECTUAL PROPERTY

The second major challenge for your legal advisers can be the cause of heartburn and sleepless nights. If your business model is dependent on intellectual property (IP) protection—whether it's trademarks or patents—you must be able to protect that IP in your new market, because any protections you have in the United States don't apply outside our borders.

There are two main challenges with protecting IP in other markets, the first of which is simply finding out how to begin the process. Your legal team must sort out what it takes to file, obtain, and maintain a trademark or patent in each new market you intend to enter.

Then a bigger problem may arise. In some world markets, even if you have legal protection for your IP, it may still be difficult to protect it on a practical level. In countries such as China, the general attitude is that IP theft is a cost of doing business in that country. As we saw with Tom in the introduction, it's not unusual in China for businesses to be created that are based on existing product designs and IP from other countries.

Luckily, the Chinese market is moving toward better protection, in part because China has begun to develop IP of its own and recognizes the importance of protection as an incentive for people to develop more of it. But the challenge for foreign companies remains.

In countries such as China that use character-based languages, there's also the issue of protecting trade names that originated in the English language. You'll have to decide if you're filing to protect the meanings of certain words or phonetic sounds, which is further complicated by the fact that you're dealing with a foreign language and culture.

I'm sure you can see now why I said these challenges can result in heartburn and sleepless nights. It's important to tackle them early in the process.

Your legal people will face other challenges that are hopefully less formidable. For instance, most foreign countries have something equivalent to an American antitrust law. This affects things like dealer protection and price discrimination. It can impact your ability to enforce exclusive territories with dealers and distributors.

Most countries also have franchise regulations, much as we do in the United States. These regulations restrict or dictate how a company can go about creating, offering, and managing franchise opportunities. If your business falls into that category, there's another legal aspect you'll have to familiarize yourselves with before setting up shop.

Tax policy is another hurdle your legal team will need to clear. They'll need to know how income on sales of product gets recognized in other countries, as well as where the tax liability sits. They'll have to know how to arrange your foreign sales in a way that minimizes your exposure to confiscatory tax regimes, if you're operating in a country that would take more of your money than you'd like for them to take. They'll also need to understand how a value-added tax (VAT) is applied and administered, because VAT is used in many other countries around the world.

While not exhaustive, this list should give you an idea of the laws your legal support should consider in your new market. Keep in mind the resources mentioned in chapter 4 if you need help with a regulatory landscape that is radically different from ours.

EXPECTATIONS AROUND INTERNATIONAL TRAVEL

Just as there will be a new array of legal issues to deal with, you'll also need to plan for different human resource challenges to transition into a foreign culture and to ensure your company culture remains healthy. The first relates to travel, as once your company sets up shop abroad, you'll have people flying to international destinations.

Most businesses have travel policies of some kind, and those will be challenged here as the question of expense becomes a larger issue. Many companies understandably require people to fly at the lowest possible fare. It's fine to sit in coach and get off the plane in Indianapolis and go visit a customer, but what about when your rep lands in Asia after flying across twelve time zones? They might be staying in a hotel with unfamiliar amenities, eating strange food, and dealing with severe jet lag. Suddenly, the lowest fare doesn't seem like the best choice if they're expected to quickly turn around and meet with customers after getting off that flight and stepping into a foreign environment.

Some businesses permit their international people to book more expensive seats so the traveler can get more work done and get some sleep during the flight. But once off the plane, they may still be required to go directly to a meeting. This solution works for some companies, but your company's management will need to determine if this added expense is necessary and can be afforded as part of the international effort.

Other companies manage this issue by requiring employees to be in the country for a couple of days to get over their jet lag before starting substantial negotiations. Of course, there's a cost there in terms of time and paying for extra nights in a hotel. The trick is finding the right balance for your company. Whatever path works best, your company's new travel policy will need to be made very clear to employees so they know exactly what is expected when navigating international travel.

Another aspect of a company's travel policy is safety. That's not to suggest that other countries are inherently unsafe or less safe than the United States, but there are health issues and emergency situations for which your company should prepare. One example is ensuring that employees have the necessary immunizations before traveling abroad.

While emergency situations are unlikely to happen, it's important to prepare for them, especially if you're doing business in a country that has demonstrated hostility toward American businesspeople. Consider if your company should carry executive hostage insurance, which many large companies now carry. Again, this isn't meant to scare you off doing business internationally but to help you prepare for a worst-case scenario.

The best way to keep your employees safe is to educate them on any risks they might face and how to safeguard themselves from potential safety issues. Don't be the company that ends up with a nightmare scenario on its hands because it failed to adequately train its employees on best safety practices in foreign countries.

As a starting point, the State Department issues travel safety alerts for American citizens traveling abroad. These tend to be general, but if you're going to start looking at markets, you and your HR staff should be aware of any pertinent warnings. In most cases, the best strategy is to be humble, stay inconspicuous, and remain aware of your surroundings.

You will also want to plan to handle medical emergencies that might arise. You'll need to evaluate the safety challenges in new markets and find ways to ensure your people stay safe when they travel.

MANAGING FOREIGN PERSONNEL

Beyond travel, there are human resource implications in hiring personnel abroad. There are legal, cultural, and practical issues involved in that process.

When hiring a foreign salesperson or customer service rep, you'll need to know the local labor laws. Can a foreign company hire someone directly? Some countries require foreign companies to set up a subsidiary in that country or work with a locally licensed entity to hire employees.

There are also laws regarding minimum wage, benefits, sick leave, vacation, severance, and more. Your company will need to get familiar with the details.

In addition to the legality involved with hiring foreign personnel, there are also cultural issues to consider. For example, what kind of incentives work with employees in your new market? The United States tends to be an individual-oriented culture. We use incentives like "Employee of the Month" or temporary access to the prime parking space to reward individual achievement and call attention to someone's exemplary work.

But in group-oriented cultures, which you'll find in many parts of Asia, it is a disincentive to single someone out from the group. This could even be perceived as a sort of frightening challenge rather than an incentive. You must be aware of these cultural differences to motivate foreign employees appropriately.

Additionally, you will want to instill in foreign employees an affinity for your company's value and an understanding of its culture. Within this task lies a potential hurdle, as some company cultures clash with the culture of the country. Take, for example, the idea of work-life balance. Spending more time at work than with your family may be perceived as noble in one culture and unacceptable in another.

You need to be aware of these potential conflicts and be able to create a balance between getting people to buy into and integrate with your company's culture, while still respecting the local culture of the people you're hiring.

Last among human resource issues, you may need to quell fears of outsourcing employees of the existing business. Again, this comes down to communication. If the VP of a successful American company jets off to China to pursue a new market opportunity, that's most likely a positive sign for the company's health and its growth outlook.

However, if management has not communicated the intent of this trip—or the company's larger goals—you can bet there will be murmurs in the cubicles about outsourcing jobs to China. This is an unfortunate side effect of today's business environment.

Statistics show that companies that do business abroad ultimately grow their domestic business as a result, even if they hire a lot of foreign employees. Most workers don't know this. For them, it's a distraction when the higher-ups travel to other countries. Instead of optimism, you get lost productivity and growing unease among employees.

The solution is to develop a communication plan and implement it in advance of any international expansion efforts. This communication should not only be informative but also motivational. Remind employees how exciting it is that the company is ready to seize new market opportunities. This will help your company culture remain positive.

TAKING THE MEASURE OF SUCCESS

Nothing has the potential to damage your company culture quite like the failure of a new business venture. You can prepare to be export-ready and cover your bases with legal and human resources, but ultimately, if you put time and money into a new effort and it flops, morale will take a big hit. Far too many companies, however, use the wrong measures of success for their international efforts and receive an inaccurate picture of how their business is doing.

Every well-run business has a few metrics they follow. These are their canaries in the coal mine, so to speak. They indicate if what the company is doing is working, or if adjustments are needed. When pursuing an international market, it might be necessary to change those metrics so as not to underestimate the success your company is having, or conversely, miss key red flags in time to correct the course.

In a sense, each new market is like a startup business. Startups have different metrics. If you don't take that into account and simply apply your existing company metrics to this new endeavor, you're not going to be measuring the right things. It will be more difficult to tell if your company is succeeding in this new venture or having problems, and if there are problems, discerning what adjustments need to be made.

Keep in mind that it took time to grow sales and achieve profitability in your domestic market. The same will be true of your new market. Starting out, you'll have additional expenses as you do things like create new literature and bring on new salespeople. Make sure the accounting department attributes these new expenses to the new venture and not your existing business. The same is true for inventory—attribute new inventory to the market expansion. Increased inventory shouldn't affect incentives for domestic workers. This is fair, and it encourages cooperation regarding the company's international goals.

When it comes to profit, there are two important equations to keep in mind:

Margin = Income/Sales
Velocity = Sales/Assets

In a new market, the key is to decide what you want to drive first and understand how that will affect your return. If you increase your inventory (assets), you will need to increase your sales to maintain a high velocity. At the same time, you can't lower your price to chase sales because that will lower your income and, ultimately, your profits. Remember that your sales reps must sell the value of your product, not its price. Sales are great, but not if you've lowered your price so you are selling more product but not making enough money doing it.

When you sell based on value, you can justify a higher price point.

Sometimes it can take years for companies to find sustained success in a new market. Whatever your company is selling, be sure to adjust your measures for success abroad. Eventually, your international endeavor should develop into a more mature business that can be measured with your existing metrics. Until then, don't jump the gun and deem something a failure because you went in with unrealistic expectations.

As we conclude, I don't want you to miss a key point about the issues we've discussed in this chapter and the last one. The challenges around issues such as extending credit, complying with export regulations, and modifying your packaging for international shipment won't be completely solved during the planning process. They are included in these two chapters because you need to plan for them, but it doesn't end once you're selling in a new market.

In fact, that's when these issues will require more of your focus than ever. As your company deals with problems you never could have anticipated during the planning phase, your approach to mitigating these issues will undoubtedly change. I wanted to make you aware of them now, so you can keep them in mind throughout this entire process.

Having considered these challenges and made initial preparations, it's time to fully enter your new international market. One of your first goals should be to build relationships with reputable businesspeople with whom you can share sustained, mutual success.

SECTION III

MARKET PENETRATION: RELATIONSHIPS, LONG-TERM PLANNING, AND MARKET-ENTRY VEHICLES

CHAPTER 7

PEOPLE AND CULTURE, NOT CONTRACTS

The first deal I ever did in China taught me an important lesson.

My team and I were in the process of purchasing a manufacturing plant there. We had done quite a bit of due diligence, including having engineers inspect the plant and making some trips over there to look at it ourselves. We'd also done a lot of work on the supply chain and logistics side of things to get the right supply of raw materials. We had familiarized ourselves with labor issues concerning who was working there currently and how many people we needed. We felt confident we had an excellent grasp of the situation.

We'd also spent an extensive amount of time drawing up

what we intended to be the purchase contract. There were long phone calls with different lawyers from around the world, including a lawyer from Washington, DC, researching compliance questions and a lawyer from Shanghai who gave us the Chinese point of view. No expense was spared. On one call, I'd estimate we had lawyers worth a combined $3,000 an hour on the phone.

We tackled tricky details that would make an ordinary person chew their arm off, torturing ourselves over questions such as stand-alone versus subordinate clauses. In the end, we came up with a pretty solid document that we felt good about. It seemed to address all the issues on both sides and was about ten pages long, which, all things considered, was fairly concise. This document would serve as an initial letter of intent that would eventually lead to the final purchase agreement once we'd addressed the substantive issues covered in it.

A group of us flew to China for a big signing ceremony followed by a banquet. At the ceremony, we were presented with the Chinese seller's letter of intent.

It was a one-page document, entirely in Chinese.

We were certain it didn't contain everything found in our ten-page document, and because it was in Chinese, I doubted it had subordinate clauses, meaning we'd obsessed over those details unnecessarily. Nevertheless, after our Chinese team member in Shanghai had read it, she assured us it did a good job of capturing the gist of the document we had so carefully crafted.

We signed it, and the letter became our contract at that point in the deal.

A CONTRACT CALLED A CONTRACT IS NOT A CONTRACT

It turned out that we were right to sign the document despite its brevity. We weren't being cheated or duped—the Chinese simply have a different idea than Americans do about what a contract really is, and for them, it has everything to do with relationships.

The US legal system is highly developed. We tend to put business deals together using strategically negotiated, carefully crafted documents. This gives us a sense of confidence and security. But not every culture is like this. In some situations, you'll be doing deals where the contract looks like nothing you've ever put together. If it's in another language, you yourself may not be able to read a word of it. The best you'll have is the assurance from one of your people who speaks the language that it's close to the general idea.

What I experienced during my first deal in China perfectly shows the Chinese attitude toward contracts. In their culture, contracts are guidelines. They are a way of capturing the current state of your relationship, but relationships evolve. Why be so terribly hung up on this one specific point in time? Our Chinese associates opted for a one-page letter instead of an elaborate document, because relationships aren't set in stone.

One of the underlying foundations of Chinese culture is the Tao or the *Tao Te Ching*. I have a version of it that translates the first verse as, "Tao called Tao is not Tao." I believe this summarizes the Chinese attitude toward contracts. A contract called a contract is not a contract, because the contract is the *relationship*, not the piece of paper.

For Americans, it can be nerve-wracking to place everything on that trust, but ultimately, you come to realize, as I did, that it's not the contracts that help you sleep at night. Instead, it's knowing you have good relationships with your business partners and associates. You trust them, and they trust you. You're confident your interests are aligned, and you're supporting each other to achieve the same result.

We'll look at negotiation strategies in a later chapter, but it's fair to say we could all benefit from thinking more like the Taoists. Ultimately, whether you're doing business domestically or with people half a world away who speak a different language, you build a relationship. It's not about a piece of paper; it's about doing business with people you can trust.

IT'S ABOUT TIME

If the importance of trust is a universal trait in business, there are more specific cultural differences that could cause a lot of misunderstandings and friction if you don't expect or understand them. One of the biggest of these for American businesspeople is the way some cultures view time and its various dimensions. Several aspects of time will come up repeatedly as you start to do business in other cultures. One is what I call the importance of precise time—that is, simply staying on schedule.

In the United States, we prefer a calendar-based approach to time. If you have a meeting at 11:00 a.m., you're expected to be there at 11:00 a.m. If that's not possible, you'll let people know as far in advance as you can, and you'd better have a good excuse. This is particularly true if, for example, you're dealing with someone who is flying into the country to meet with you.

On the other hand, some countries have a different perception of time, and they handle it much differently than Americans. To use sociological terms, the American culture tends to look at time sequentially. Other cultures may take a more synchronistic approach.

In cultures where relationships are of central importance, people are more concerned with being where they are now than where they're supposed to be next. Their full focus is on the person they're meeting with, not the next person on their schedule. If the person they're with is important, it won't bother them to run late and miss another appointment.

In their mind, the next obligation begins once the current one is complete. It doesn't happen at some arbitrary time you set three weeks ago, when you didn't know what would be happening on that day. If this means they return to their office at 2:00 p.m. even though you were there for the scheduled 11:00 a.m. meeting, that's your problem.

Not understanding this difference can create tension. I speak from experience, as this has happened to me in Mexico and some Asian countries, too. Each time I would arrive before our meeting, only to be told the person I was supposed to meet wasn't in the office. I'd cool my jets in the waiting room and wait for a couple of hours. Finally, an assistant would tell me matter-of-factly that tomorrow would be better, even though I flew there just for this meeting, booked one night in a hotel, and had a return flight scheduled for the next day.

You feel like you're being taken advantage of, but that's most likely not the case. It's simply a cultural difference that most Americans have never experienced.

Another time-related issue is the way different cultures view short-term and long-term planning. When an American business outlines a long-term strategic plan, they're usually looking three to five years out. They make that plan knowing full well it'll be outdated in five years and will need to be redone. Typically, the American business culture is more focused on short-term results—this month, quarter, and year. Any company that can look past that and put together a three-year strategy is ahead of the game.

In countries such as Japan, long term is fifty years.

This can result in complications when you deal with other cultures depending on how you feel about their perspective. It's a problem if you don't appreciate it, but it's an opportunity if you do appreciate it. American business-people tend to go into a deal focused first and foremost on what they're going to get out of it now and in the next six to twelve months. If we can't be successful in that short-term horizon, we'd say it's probably not a good deal. On the other hand, someone with a cultural mindset like the Japanese will go into the deal wondering where it will leave them in fifteen, twenty, and fifty years.

You can see this as a huge disconnect, but I see it as an opportunity. Achieving near-term objectives and considering a situation from a long-term perspective may not be mutually exclusive. It's possible you can address what's most important to the other party and what's most important to you without coming into conflict if you're mindful of the different time frames that are in play. When you do that, you create a win-win situation.

However, this difference can create tension in unexpected ways. Let's continue with the example of someone from the United States doing business with someone from Japan. If you talk to American businesspeople who have negotiated deals there, they'll probably have a similar story to the one I'll describe here. Your organization flies team members to Japan for a weeklong visit to help move a deal along. They have a flight home scheduled for Friday, and by the morning of that flight, they feel confident that significant progress has been made. Suddenly, as your team prepares to head to the airport, the Japanese throw a curveball into the deal.

With that one conversation, it feels like all the progress your team has made over the past week has melted away. As Americans, it would be easy to feel like we're being played in that situation. Your team has a decision to make—walk away entirely, cancel the flight, stay in Japan to resolve this new issue, or schedule a return trip at a later date.

The answer comes down to how patient you're willing to be to make the deal happen.

The mistake here would be to view this as a sneaky negotiation tactic employed by your Japanese associates. That's certainly part of it—the Japanese are savvy and know how Americans operate—but it's more about their view of time than trying to gain an advantage in the negotiations. When your long-term view is fifty years, another couple of months of negotiation or a second trip to Japan to finish things up is no big deal.

The pressure in situations like these is self-inflicted. When your team is expected to come back with a finished deal in hand so the company can start selling product in Japan within six months, needing another trip to close the deal can feel like the end of the world. In these high-stakes situations, attitudes can turn sour quickly. The Americans see the Japanese as sneaky for moving the goalpost at the last minute, while the Japanese see the Americans as dumb for having such a shortsighted view of things.

In chapter 9, we'll examine how misunderstandings can ruin good relationships and how you can keep that from happening, but in this context, the key is patience. You will struggle to build relationships or complete negotiations with foreign partners if you default to the American ideas of short-term and long-term planning. When you show the other party that you can see things from their viewpoint, trust is built on both sides.

Another aspect of time where cultures can differ is the concept of busyness. In the United States and most Northern European cultures, we strive to constantly be doing something that moves the metaphorical ball farther down the field. We get uncomfortable when things aren't happening. It's not enough to just "be." We must "do." For better or worse, this idea drives the workplace experience. I say "worse" because sometimes this idea backfires and employees are expected to look busy, even if they're not accomplishing anything.

But in many cultures, being busy is not important. It's being thoughtful that matters. The idea of "being" is more important than "doing." That's why these cultures place a greater value on where they are now as opposed to where they're supposed to be next.

When you're concerned about busyness, you tend to get caught up in the urgent, which can be detrimental. Instead of sitting back and looking at the big picture, urgency makes us spend our time running from one problem to the next, putting out fires all day. Americans like to say they focus on what's important, not what's urgent. But our inclination toward busyness often causes us to do the opposite. In many other cultures, however, there is not that disincentive to focus on the important. These cultures are more driven by the long-term future, which frees them up to build relationships in the here and now.

When Americans open themselves up to this idea of being thoughtful as opposed to being busy, it can be quite liberating. You get the chance to leave the over-worked, urgent environment we usually occupy and spend some time looking at the big picture. It would be tough for most American companies to do this consistently, but when they do business in other countries where this mindset is prevalent, my hope is they would slow down and see things from a new point of view. It will foster a better understanding of their new business partners and strengthen that burgeoning relationship. Not to mention, it will allow them to "be" for a moment. Doesn't that sound nice?

THE CULTURAL CHALLENGE OF COMMUNICATION

Time is not the only challenge that can hinder your ability to build relationships within your new international market. Just like in the United States, communication is vital to building trust and understanding with other people. The challenge is that people in every country communicate differently. When we fail to understand these differences, we can't anticipate their impact on our business, and relationships can quickly sour.

Language, of course, can be an issue, but this runs deeper. Communication is about how you share information. As Americans, we prefer a direct style of communication. We'd rather cut to the chase and say what we mean, even if what we're saying is negative.

This preference shows up in a big way during negotiations. Sure, we'll feel each other out at first, but once we've sized the other party up, we're eager to get to the bottom line. We want this, and you want that. Can we make a deal happen? If so, let's do it. If not, let's move on. The same is true with presentations. We want the important data, not the fluff.

In countries with a direct communication style, truth is a matter of empirical fact. Truth is quantifiable, which means with a little research, you can tell whether another person is lying to you or not. We place a high priority on telling and being told the truth.

Cultures with a contextual communication style don't share this point of view. In these cultures, a higher priority is placed on maintaining the relationship than on stating the factual truth. The implication is that you can't have an important conversation in contextual cultures until you've established understanding with someone, which takes time.

In international business, you'll spend a great deal of

time sitting around discussing the weather, family, and other topics you didn't fly across the globe to discuss. The other person isn't trying to waste your time; they're trying to build a relationship that will make the ensuing conversations more meaningful. You might be tempted to cut to the chase, but you should avoid giving in to that temptation. In instances like these, jumping the gun can actually be detrimental to achieving the goals you sat down to achieve.

This can be a frustrating situation for American business-people or for someone from a contextual culture who's trying to do business with us. It's why they find us rude and abrupt, and we find them evasive.

To help develop this contextual understanding, there are very specific markers to be aware of for each culture. For example, in China, as in many Asian cultures, it is impolite to directly tell someone no. Think about how hard it is to say no to someone we love and care about when they really want something. If a relationship is important, saying no isn't going to help it grow. It may even end it. It's not that people from contextual cultures don't say no; they just express it in an indirect, softer way.

Let's look at an example of a conversation between an American businessperson and a Chinese supplier to see how this can play out. The American needs an order shipped within a tight time frame, and as he attempts to communicate that to his Chinese supplier, he misses the subtle ways the supplier attempts to tell him no. Here's how the conversation begins.

American buyer: "We need the order shipped by the end of the month."

Chinese supplier: "It will be a challenge, but we will do everything we can to make you an important and happy customer."

The American is directly expressing what he needs. If we understand the contextual culture the Chinese supplier comes from, we can read between the lines to see his true response. "You know, it's a challenge. I don't see it happening. But the important thing is our relationship, and we're going to do everything we can to let you know you're important and ultimately make you happy. After all, that's what really counts."

A few weeks later, the American hasn't heard from the supplier, and the American is feeling a little uneasy.

American buyer: "Are we on schedule? Are we all good on our order?"

Chinese supplier: "Don't worry. Your order is being

worked on, so it is on our schedule. And yes, we are good."

In this conversation, the supplier is mirroring and affirming the American's words, but by not outright agreeing with him, he's also implying that yes, the company is working on the order, but it may not be on the American's schedule.

Finally, things are getting down to the wire, and they have another conversation.

American buyer: "Will our order be shipped as we agreed?"

Chinese supplier: "Your order is to be shipped, of course."

American buyer: "But by the end of the month?"

Chinese supplier: "That is requiring more employees and more shifts."

American buyer: "Whatever it takes. You understand?"

Chinese supplier: "Yes, I can understand what you say."

This is where the American completely misses what the

supplier is saying. By saying that filling the order on time requires more employees and more shifts, he's also saying it's not going to happen, because he doesn't have the resources. But the American is hearing the reassurance that even if it requires more employees and more shifts, it will get done.

This conversation perfectly illustrates the differences between direct and contextual communication styles. The American wants a yes or no answer, and the Chinese supplier, given that he values the relationship, won't tell the American no.

Sadly, when the shipment doesn't arrive on time in this pretend scenario, the American will feel like he's been lied to, and the Chinese supplier will be exhausted from dealing with an American who failed to hear no every time they talked. The way to avoid this situation is to recognize the communication style of your new market. You'll need to adjust your expectations around how business gets done when relationships are the priority.

RELATIONSHIPS ARE KEY TO YOUR EFFORTS ABROAD

When you do business abroad, you should strive to build successful long-term relationships based on knowledge, trust, and understanding. Your success in foreign markets will be entirely dependent on building these types of relationships, which means you'll need patience and understanding if you hope to be successful.

Good relationships, whether in business or not, take time to build. When there are different cultures involved, the time required goes up significantly. You're also guaranteed to have miscommunications with your foreign contacts along the way. If you allow it, these mix-ups can sabotage your efforts to build trust and understanding in your new relationships.

When you're dealing with superior businesspeople in your market, what you must remember is that miscommunication stems from cultural differences, not nefarious behavior by the other party. Don't look for fault when things get misunderstood or negotiations take an unexpected turn. You're conducting business in a cultural context that's different from the American way of doing business.

There will be some bumps in the road, but they don't have to throw you off track. Stay focused on building strong relationships and things will get easier as you go.

Now, I hope you didn't miss the key phrase that's the lynchpin of this entire argument: superior businesspeople in your new market. I'm not talking about taking your lumps to maintain a relationship with someone whose shady behavior jeopardizes your business. I never would've advised Tom to keep working with the distributor who exposed his company to liability issues and eventually ripped off his product.

If you run across behavior like that, then end the relationship immediately. Or better yet, don't get involved with an individual or organization like that in the first place. Focus on finding people and groups in your new market that are reputable and share goals like yours.

How do you find these people, you ask? Let's dive into the next chapter and find out.

CHAPTER 8

WHOM TO MEET AND HOW TO MEET THEM

We've established that relationships hold the key to your success in international markets, but only if those relationships are with superior businesspeople. From this truth emerges two questions: what characteristics do these people have, and how do you meet them?

If you're attending trade shows, you'll meet plenty of nice, funny people in your field. Among them might be the perfect contact for launching your business in a new market. But you've got to look deeper than someone's personality. Just because you enjoy getting dinner or drinks with someone doesn't mean they're the right business partner. They could be—it's entirely possible they have all the characteristics we'll discuss in this chapter.

It's also possible they're the wrong kind of partner—they can't help your business succeed or, worse, want to steal your idea and make a knockoff version of your product.

You may get only one chance at going international, which places paramount importance on finding the right foreign partners from the start. You're looking for superior businesspeople to work with, and those people have the following four characteristics:

1. They have knowledge of the market and access to customers.
2. They share your goals and believe in what you're doing.
3. They will succeed when you succeed.
4. They act ethically.

Let's look at how these characteristics will help enable your success in a new market.

QUALITIES OF SUPERIOR BUSINESSPEOPLE

The first and most important criteria to use when assessing potential foreign contacts are knowledge of the market and access to customers. You know your product. What you lack is in-depth knowledge of this new market, including who the customers are, where they hang out, and the cultural barriers that block you from connecting with them and gaining their trust. If the contact you're considering does not possess knowledge and access, move on—they can't help your business succeed in this new market.

One of your first connections will likely be a sales rep, distributor, or someone in a similar position. People in these positions tend to know the market and have access to customers, which make them a logical target for an early business contact. With them, you can clear what is usually the biggest hurdle to success in a foreign market.

The second characteristic is a belief in what your company is trying to accomplish, which often comes when you have shared goals. Your measuring stick here should be your company's value proposition—does this person innately understand it? Can they explain it to a customer in such a way that it resonates with their worldview?

Foreign sales reps must pass this test. You've priced your product or service at a point that allows you to be successful and competitive, but if your value proposition isn't understood, this sales rep will keep telling you to lower your price. You don't need partners who can sell your product; you need partners who can sell your value proposition. When customers push back on price, your local agent's answer should be, "Let me explain the value," rather than, "Let me call my supplier to see if they'll drop the price."

When businesspeople in your new market share the same

goals as your company, they're more likely to understand and believe in your value proposition. They're trying to get to the same place you are, which sets up the potential for a win-win scenario. This is the third characteristic of superior businesspeople—they succeed when you succeed. Common interests form a solid foundation for a strong working relationship. That said, it's important to start with the first two characteristics, as this one tends to naturally follow the others.

I want to add an important caveat here. If you find someone who possesses these characteristics, they might be a superior businessperson, but that doesn't mean they're automatically the right person to help your business. You must always be ready to walk away from a bad deal, no matter how much time or energy you've invested in building that relationship. There are always more contacts out there, and we'll look at how to find them.

You don't have to burn bridges—maybe the next time you're back there, you'll have drinks. But if you can't agree on a deal that works for both sides, walk away and keep looking.

HOW TO MEET THE RIGHT PEOPLE

I'm always amazed by American businesspeople who attempt to break into a new market without knowing anyone. Like Tom, they'll blindly search for someone at a trade show and most likely end up settling for someone they enjoy being around. They have no idea the criteria they should use for judging potential business relationships, so they end up in situations where their contacts are unknowingly sabotaging their international efforts.

The good news is that there are ways to connect with superior businesspeople before you ever leave the country. The organizations I've mentioned throughout the book—the USEAC, US Department of Agriculture (USDA), and the World Trade Centers Association (WTCA)—can all assist in your search. In addition, we'll look at how associations such as Rotary International can help, as well as the role private consultants play in this process.

Let's talk about the USEAC first, because it offers a service that's one of the best-kept secrets of the international business world: the Gold Key Service.

The first step is to meet with someone at your local USEAC office. Most major US cities have offices, and each office has staff members who are experts on certain markets. For example, if you're interested in doing business in Hong Kong, you can meet with the staffer focused on developing business in Asia. They'll ask you questions to assess the nature of your business, your value proposition, and your business needs.

Once they have this information, they can determine the type of person you need to connect with to break into Hong Kong, be it a sales rep, distributor, or foreign business owner. Using their local connections, the staffer will compile a list of contacts and will do some initial vetting for you. They'll run background checks and consider credit worthiness, reputation in the industry, and other factors to determine if this person is the real deal.

The result will be a shortlist of up to five candidates worth your consideration. They can also guide you in arranging your travel to Hong Kong, and they will facilitate the meetings.

The Gold Key Service is advantageous if you're serious about a new market. You'll meet with people who've been vetted by professionals with your best interests in mind. Your introduction to them will be facilitated by people who carry some weight in the local market; you're not just someone showing up cold. The USEAC can also provide other resources you might need to facilitate these meetings, including interpreters.

You'd think the cost of this service would be exorbitant, but it's accessibly priced for businesses of all sizes. If you're a small company, the cost is just $950. For medium-sized companies, it's $2,300, and for large companies, it's only $3,400. The USEAC requires your company to be export-ready, but if you are, this is a small price to pay for a golden opportunity to get connected with superior businesspeople in your new market.

Other US government agencies have resources that can help you find the right person overseas as well. This is true even on a state level. Most states have an office of international trade or economic development that help companies from that state.

One agency I'd recommend is the USDA. It's often overlooked because people don't realize the USDA isn't focused exclusively on farming, livestock, and produce. Furthermore, the USDA doesn't just operate in the United States. It has offices all over the world and a vast network of resources, including connections in the distribution chain. This means the agency can benefit your business even if you're not involved with agriculture. If you are, the USDA can greatly assist your international efforts.

A few years ago, I worked with people at the USDA office in Shanghai. The staff there had more knowledge and insight into online shopping platforms and consumer trends in China than anyone else I'd encountered, including the Department of Commerce. The reason they were so tuned-in was because China is ahead of the curve with online food ordering and delivery, as well as e-shopping for agricultural items. This prompted the USDA staff there to educate themselves on this phenomenon. Ultimately, they gained such a comprehensive understanding that it had applications beyond the agriculture sector.

While the Department of Commerce can help you understand and navigate political and cultural trends in a market, I've found that the USDA staff usually knows the movers and shakers in their industry and those related to it. When you connect with someone in that office, in addition to general advice, you may hear, "I know this person. I had dinner with him and his family last week. Let's set up a time we can meet at his office."

Even better, the staff member will probably say it with enthusiasm. The USDA staff I've worked with were incredibly friendly and approachable people who seemed genuinely excited that an American businessperson came to their office asking for help.

If there are any major land grant universities in your area, you can use them to connect with the USDA office best equipped to help you make headway in your new market.

We've looked at the WTCA and its perks already, but it's worth revisiting here to discuss how the association can assist you with this process. There are more than three hundred World Trade Centers around the world, and they are located in almost every major city. Each one may have a slightly different focus, but they're all networked together. Whether the office is a real estate player, such as Manila, or provides real-world training, such as Denver, the cumulative reach of this organization can't be over-stated when it comes to international business.

Becoming a member could be beneficial to your business, especially if there's an office in the international market you've targeted. You'll have access to more than fifteen thousand professionals across the globe who can provide guidance, ongoing training on topics such as foreign regulations and export compliance, and a vast network of partners who can make introductions or point you toward good opportunities.

I'm admittedly biased, but there's no denying the ways the WTCA can help your business.

Rotary International is a business organization that's present in more than two hundred countries and counts about 1.2 million members worldwide. As you can imagine, it can also be an excellent resource for networking at home and overseas.

A major advantage of Rotary International is that it's particularly popular in some places that are hard for businesses to break into such as India. I can personally attest to this, having worked with a company that made their connection to a distributor in India through their activity and relationships in Rotary International.

Because it's a business-focused organization, it attracts the type of people you're looking for: those who are active in their business community and have connections that could help you. If someone at your company is involved with Rotary, utilize this resource.

Finally, private consultants can also help you make connections abroad. In fact, the organizations we just discussed can introduce you to the right consultant for your business.

One advantage to using a private consultant is working with a professional who is laser focused on a specific market and possesses a deeper knowledge than someone responsible for a large geographic area like Southeast Asia. If they're worth their fee, a consultant will know superior businesspeople to connect you with, plus they will help you navigate the cultural norms discussed in the previous chapter to begin building those relationships.

Good consultants can provide you with valuable knowledge about niche industries and make you aware of specialized details like regulatory compliance strategies. For example, I worked with a Colorado-based, American consultant who had lived and worked in China for many years. He spoke fluent Chinese and focused on helping American food companies access the Chinese market. He doesn't look for general clients, but if your business falls into his niche, he could provide you with tremendous insight and access.

Obviously, a downside with private consultants is the cost, especially compared to the other resources I've mentioned, which are free or affordable for most companies. Hiring a consultant may come down to your business size and commitment to your international endeavor. But it's an option that's worth considering if you want to make the right international connections.

All the resources mentioned in this chapter offer a great deal of valuable information, networking opportunities, and specialized guidance. The key is finding the best fit to help your business make the right connections in your international market of choice.

In these last couple of chapters, we've looked at the reasons why relationships are crucial to your international success, and the superior businesspeople you should seek to connect with in your new market. Once you've found those people, you'll need to develop a strong relationship that's built to last, which is the focus of the next chapter.

CHAPTER 9

TRUST: BUILDING QUALITY RELATIONSHIPS THAT LAST

Once you've found superior businesspeople in your new market who are a good fit for your business, you'll need to develop those relationships. The first step is developing some degree of cultural understanding—you must know how to relate to your new associates, so you can work together effectively. Developing a relationship with a foreign sales rep will probably require more patience than developing a relationship with a distributor in South Bend, Indiana, because of this need for cultural acumen. But it's a worthwhile, necessary investment. Understanding each other will help build mutual trust and confidence. Ultimately, that trust is what will allow you to sleep at night.

With this understanding assured, you must work to establish and maintain a mutually beneficial relationship. The goal is to create a win-win situation where if you succeed, so does your foreign partner. This will keep you both moving forward in the same direction.

Part of creating a win-win situation comes from negotiating a fair deal for both sides. As we've seen, negotiating deals in foreign countries can look different than it does in the United States.

NEGOTIATION TACTICS FOR FOREIGN MARKETS

Being a good negotiator can help you close business deals. The negotiation strategies and skills you've honed at home, however, will get you only so far when it comes to a foreign market where you're in an unfamiliar setting trying to negotiate across cultures.

As with any negotiation, you'll want to enter foreign talks with an understanding of where your contact wants to end up, where you need to end up, and any possible deal breakers. You need to know all the things you're able to sacrifice and what you need to get from the deal. The other side will have its own idea of what a fair deal looks like that has been shaped by its company, country, and culture.

Keep in mind that different cultures have varying ideas of

what's valuable. If what is considered valuable is different for you and your partner, your overall goals may differ as well. Ethical principles also vary across cultures. You and your negotiation partner may vary on what is considered fair, and on how acceptable it is to insist, advocate, or exaggerate. From our discussion in chapter 7, you can't assume that you share the same views on objective "truth" as the person across the table.

When you're "playing on the road" (i.e., traveling to another country for negotiations), there are a multitude of issues that'll add to your stress. To begin with, there are the immediate, physical challenges, such as dealing with jet lag, unfamiliar accommodations, and food. Then there are issues like transportation arrangements and technology problems, including making sure your cell phone will work and whether you can connect with your team back home.

When you finally arrive at the meeting place, you'll have to consider the setup of the room and whether you're speaking with the person in charge or merely an emissary (in which case, you'll have to work your way up the line). Even if communication is clear with your contact, you may have issues reaching your organization back home. For example, during negotiations, you might need to check with support personnel at your home office to make sure something is possible. You may be negotiating in the middle of the day where you are, but it could be 2:00 a.m. for the person you're trying to reach.

Added to all this is a pressure that you might feel to conclude a deal prematurely, because you're worried about compounding travel expenses and time away from the home office. The reality is that it takes longer to negotiate a deal in a foreign country, often for cultural reasons, but also because the other party knows of your travel limitations. If you're working with superior businesspeople, they're savvy enough to push that button, if needed. Yes, there are teleconferencing apps that can be used to finish incomplete deals from the comfort of your conference room back home, but when you've traveled across the world to close a deal in person, there's often a self-imposed pressure to finish it before you come home. Don't take a bad deal just for the sake of time. Additional travel expenses are far less expensive than the cost you could incur by hurriedly agreeing to a bad deal.

The best way to deal with these challenges is to have a detailed plan going into the negotiations. When you arrive, know how you'll coordinate with support personnel back home, the technology you'll have access to, and whether you'll need a day or two to deal with jet lag and get a lay of the land before negotiations begin.

You'll also need to adjust your attitude. Understand that

negotiating in a foreign country requires more patience if you want to do it right. Remember that you're not just bartering a deal; you're developing a relationship with your business contact. If you're in a contextual culture, that relationship takes precedent over getting a signed piece of paper.

Considering these challenges, you may wonder if it's better to bring your foreign contacts to your home office to negotiate, instead of going to them. There's a theory of negotiation that holds that if the person is coming to you, you get the control. You set up the room and dictate where the other party can go if they need to have a sidebar or make a call. You control the lighting, temperature, food, and the interruptions.

What I've found after years of negotiating deals both domestically and abroad, however, is there's a problem with this idea. When it comes to negotiation, the biggest barrier to success is the ability to make the other side feel comfortable with the deal. Therein lies the advantage of going to play on the other team's turf. They are in their element, feeling comfortable. This means they might be more open to certain compromises. If the discomfort of being in an unfamiliar place had been a factor, the other party might not be as receptive to whatever compromises you're asking them to make.

When you think about it, most cultures around the world

love hosting others. If you go to them for negotiations, your partner will want to make you comfortable, which is more likely to reinforce and promote the essential win-win, multiple-advantage mentality that comes with a superior business contact. There is an additional advantage to traveling for business as well: it can be a wonderful cultural experience.

In some situations, it makes sense to bring your foreign business partners to you for negotiations. But if you need to travel to them, don't fret. All the challenges we've covered can be overcome if you plan for the variables you might face. Be adaptable and don't get stuck thinking things have to be a certain way. Keep in mind your goals, but also consider how you can create a win-win situation for both parties.

STRUCTURE CONTRACTS TO YIELD LONG-TERM BENEFITS

In chapter 7, we looked at how different cultures perceive short-term and long-term planning, as well as how contracts are perceived differently around the world. Contracts in the international business world tend to comply more with the cultural norms of your foreign market, so these two factors will weigh heavily in the negotiations. Regardless of the cultural factors at play, everyone's goal should be to create a deal that yields the most long-term benefit to both sides. Here are a couple of strategies to ensure that happens.

FOCUS ON INCENTIVES, NOT PENALTIES

When two US companies draw up a contract, they tend to focus on disincentives or penalty clauses, spelling out what will happen if one side fails to do something. When doing international deals, however, it's better to focus on incentives.

For one thing, it's much more difficult to enforce penalties from half a world away. For another, this positive reinforcement encourages the idea of mutual success, one of the essential parts of your relationship with important overseas contacts.

TRANSLATE THE CONTRACT

I've seen a lot of contracts with a clause stipulating that the English-language version is the controlling one. Often, there isn't even a version of the contract in the other language. Either way, it's a mistake to think that making one version of a contract the official one solves a fundamental problem.

As a practical matter, the language of enforcement is always the language of the country in which a case would be tried. So if you're doing business in Japan, the language of enforcement wouldn't be English. Then there's the issue of trust and mutual respect, which is upheld by translating your contracts into both languages. Choosing a controlling language isn't important. What is important is that each version expresses essentially the same thing.

A strategy I use is having a contract drawn up in English, and then I get it translated into the other language. Next, I check if the other side understands the text in the contract and is comfortable with this translated version. If they are, I have it vetted through my own people to satisfy that both contracts are indeed the same on the essential components.

It may seem easier just to have someone translate the contract, but as we learned with the materials I had translated for my Mexican partners, this route is rife with pitfalls. Because so many things Americans say are contextual or idiomatic, there is no perfect literal translation. Much of our language comes from our cultural context and common usage. When something is translated exactly as it's written in English, the other party isn't going to understand it the same way we do. It may require a different nuance to communicate the same idea, the same understanding, or the same value in their language.

NOT EVERYONE SPEAKS THE SAME ENGLISH, SO USE AN INTERPRETER IF NEEDED

We've made mention of this fact throughout the book, but I want to explore it more in depth here. A common misconception among businesspeople trading internationally for the first time is that businesspeople in foreign countries speak English. This is both true and false. English is the international language of business, but it's much different than the English that Americans speak. In major cities around the world, your business interactions will be in English, but you might say something confusing to non-native English speakers.

If you step back and listen to how Americans speak, it is incredible how many idiomatic expressions we use not only every day but every hour. These ubiquitous expressions are simple things such as, "I'm going to jump in the shower." A non-native English speaker may hear this and wonder why Americans are jumping in the shower when it would be much easier to stand still while showering.

As Americans, we can mistakenly believe we're being understood in these moments because our foreign contacts will smile politely and nod along. They might even laugh half-heartedly if we say something funny. Yet, if we could read their minds, we'd see they're not really with us. If you speak a foreign language, you've probably had a similar experience where you've been talking with a native speaker and lost track. As the conversation goes on, you're not brave enough to admit you have lost the thread of the conversation.

Fortunately, there's a simple solution to any language barrier: hire an interpreter. When closing deals or building relationships abroad, these professionals provide a necessary assist.

A few years ago, I worked with someone who was trying to close a deal with a potential partner in South Korea. Both sides had hosted the other, and every time they got together, things seemed to go well. They had great conversations and a strong relationship. Yet the potential partner was never willing to pull the trigger.

I asked this person if he had ever used an interpreter.

"Well, no," he told me. "My contact speaks English pretty well."

"He does speak English well," I replied. "Relative to your Korean, he speaks amazingly well. But if you think about all the misunderstandings that could come up when you start going through specific details, he might not feel confident. He's probably on the plane headed home, worrying about the little things he didn't catch or that he felt were unclear."

I reiterated that sometimes, when dealing with a language barrier, you can get to a point of being sufficiently uncomfortable that you're just not ready to make a deal. I suggested my contact use an interpreter the next time they met. He was worried that his South Korean partner might feel insulted. This is an understandable concern, but as I explained to him, using an interpreter is the best way to approach international business deals. It's actually a sign of respect, signifying that you want to ensure both sides are on the same page.

You don't need to use an interpreter for a social interaction, such as dinner or drinks. But when you're negotiating a deal, an interpreter is an assuring presence who will guarantee that you arrive at a fundamental level of mutual understanding.

My client agreed to use an interpreter, and sure enough, it made a huge difference. In the next conversation they had, he and his contact came to an agreement.

Another essential strategy for using an interpreter is to find someone who is familiar with your industry and, if possible, with the professional relationship between you and your contact. If the interpreter you're using is not familiar with either, you need to lay some groundwork. Send them information on your company and products, as well as who the players are, who's likely to be at the negotiation, and what their interests are.

Give the interpreter enough time to read the material and ask any questions they have. If necessary, this will give them time to look up any specialized vocabulary they'll need. You want them to be comfortable interpreting in real time, especially if they encounter idiomatic expressions or industry slang. If they're comfortable with what's being said, it'll make everyone else at the table feel comfortable with the negotiations.

DEALING WITH CORRUPTION: GOOD BUSINESSPEOPLE ARE LOOKING TO DO GOOD BUSINESS

Even when you select superior businesspeople to work with in your new market, you must be aware of corruption as a potential concern. While not a common issue everywhere, it seems like every international businessperson I talk to has a story about it.

Corruption is something I feel very strongly about for several reasons, including the way it can result in the failure of your business, not only through potential legal issues but simply because of the kind of connections you'll end up dealing with if you don't avoid it.

This book is for good businesspeople who want to do things the right way when entering new international markets. In some situations, giving in to corruption can seem like the easiest way to get ahead. As the saying goes, "You go along to get along." But going along with corruption is always the wrong choice. It's a short-term fix that creates long-term problems.

Bribery is a common corrupt practice. When American companies are operating abroad, they should understand that bribing people to get business violates the Foreign Corrupt Practices Act (FCPA). Failure to abide by this law can result in significant penalties for companies doing business abroad. We're talking about fines that can run in the millions. It can also result in prison time for officers, directors, managers, and people directly involved in corrupt conduct. These may seem like good deterrents, but they're apparently not sufficient, because there are nonetheless many companies that continue to take part in corrupt activities.

Sometimes this happens due to a lack of clarity with the law. For example, there are things people generally consider corrupt that are not forbidden under the FCPA. This includes making what are called facilitation payments, which are minor payments that induce someone to do the thing they were already legally compelled to do. Think, for example, of the import control officer who's not going to stamp the piece of paper and let your shipment in unless he gets a twenty-dollar bill slipped across the table.

The FCPA is mainly focused on bribing public officials,

which presents another area in which you need to be wary. In many countries, there is a fine line between what constitutes a public official and a private official. China is a good example. There, a lot of major companies are state-owned, so people who have a corporate position may also hold a government position. It can be difficult to make the distinction, but if you're at a point where you're trying to do that, you're dealing with the wrong kinds of people.

Corrupt practices such as bribing officials are illegal in almost every country, not just the United States. Even in areas where corruption is endemic and considered a part of doing business, there are laws that make it illegal. What you need to watch out for are the ways in which corruption can be disguised as normal business activity.

These are the "wink, wink" situations where, for example, you receive an unusually high bill for "membership dues" to a certain club. Let's say you approve the payment because you're getting good results, but you don't want to think about where the money is going.

Everything seems fine until your business gets big enough that you want to take the next step. The person you've been working with isn't going to get you there, so you decide to terminate the agreement. But your partner doesn't appreciate being fired, so he contacts a local law enforcement agency about the corrupt practices of your business. Your former business partner will say that you forced them to participate or lose their job.

You can deny the charges and claim ignorance, but there's a paper trail, and now you're the foreigner being accused in a criminal system where you don't speak the language and might not fully understand the nuances of how their culture responds to crime.

This is a place you do not want to be.

In the best-case scenario, you can never return to that country again, because you'll get served with papers. In the worst-case scenario, you get served with papers and wind up making shoes in a Chinese prison for the rest of your life.

You would think these outcomes would be enough to keep American and foreign companies from engaging in corrupt behavior abroad, but it's not. For some, legal prohibitions seem to be problematic but not determinative. That said, let's close out this chapter with the ultimate imperative to avoid corruption: it's bad for business.

Avoiding corruption is about more than simply following the law and avoiding penalties and punishments. There are also many practical benefits for your business, including market differentiation and finding people with whom you truly want to do business. Avoiding corruption is a key to the fourth characteristic of superior businesspeople—acting ethically.

It's important to realize that even in markets where corruption is endemic, good businesspeople understand that corruption is bad business. In addition to legal risks, it creates inefficiencies and drives up costs.

I've done business in some of the most corrupt countries in the world and often in the construction industry, which is known for corruption even in the United States. In my experience, even in corrupt markets and industries, there are good businesspeople dying for other good businesspeople who understand the benefits of doing things the right way.

I've been there in a foreign market when your contact tells you the company won't get the big contract unless a few palms get greased. My response was always the same: "You're right, and I'm fine not getting that contract." In the short term, you will walk away from some business, but in the long term, saying no to corruption from the start will self-select the superior businesspeople in your new market. Weeding out the people who need a bribe to help your business succeed will, in fact, set your business up for long-term success. And isn't that exactly what one of your biggest unknowns is going into this whole process?

How do I find good people whom I can trust to become my business partners?

Building relationships with the right people in foreign markets will help you sleep easy at night. Whether you're negotiating a deal or enjoying a night on the town, you can best develop those relationships by seeking a mutual understanding, rather than seeing things strictly from an American perspective. Take time to understand the culture of your new market and how it might affect your interactions with people there. Remember that most negative interactions stem from cultural differences, not malicious intent.

Finally, don't give in to corruption. It will tarnish your company's reputation, end your chances for growth in that market, and damage your existing operations. In a chapter all about creating win-win situations, that's the ultimate lose-lose scenario.

In the previous chapters, we've looked at ways to research new markets, gotten your company export-ready, prepared for the impact on your company's culture, explored the qualities of worthwhile business contacts, and discovered ways to find them. The table is set for you to enter your new market, and in the final chapter, we'll examine the various market-entry vehicles to see which one best fits your company's international efforts.

CHAPTER 10

CHOOSING THE RIGHT WAY TO GO GLOCAL

When considering the best market-entry vehicle for your business, here's the fundamental question you must answer: is this a short-term or long-term play? Both routes are legitimate, but each one dictates a different path forward. Furthermore, you'll need to be prepared for what happens if a short-term play develops long-term potential. Let's look at an example to see how this process plays out for many companies.

Like a lot of businesses, Company X decides to go international after suffering a downturn in their domestic market. Many companies choose this route after a general dip in the overall economy, but for Company X, it was the loss of a major client that spurred their international interest. Using the strategies we've discussed, they begin selling to new customers in a foreign market to make up for some of their lost revenue.

Up to this point, Company X's management hasn't considered whether their international efforts are short term or long term. They're focused entirely on the fact that sales are strong, meaning the company is on its way to profitability in the new market.

After a couple of years, Company X lands a big client in their domestic market to replace the one they lost. Suddenly, the company is facing a capacity problem because the domestic demand has increased, necessitating resources that have been diverted to the new international market. The company is overextended and facing a major decision.

Will they turn a short-term play into a long-term one by adding capacity abroad to continue supporting this foreign market? Or will they cut back in either market to utilize their existing capacity in the most efficient way possible?

If they opt for the second choice, it will most likely be the international business that gets clipped, simply because it costs more to ship things halfway around the world. Scaling back or ceasing business overseas would be a practical, understandable decision, but it means cutting off everything Company X has developed abroad, including relationships they've formed with distributors and sales agents. A lot of bridges will get burned.

If the company never needs or wants to enter international markets again, maybe that doesn't matter too much. But if the market takes another downturn and Company X tries to revisit this international market in the future, they'll likely find their partners and agents abroad are inhospitable to their overtures. By failing to adequately address the scope of their efforts and communicate that with their foreign partners, Company X has forfeited the chance to return to that market.

On the other hand, Company X might opt for a long-term strategy in their foreign market. Perhaps they see global growth and diversification are key to the future success of their business, or they don't want the time and energy spent cultivating relationships with foreign partners to be wasted by shutting things down. Either way, they must now decide how to add capacity without disrupting their existing operations.

As you can see, the scope of your international efforts should be carefully considered as part of the planning process. Your company's international goals and the time frame for accomplishing them will dictate your strategy for entering and exiting the market smoothly. Even short-term plays require long-term planning if your company wants to avoid burning bridges and destroying relationships you forge overseas.

THE SPECTRUM OF MARKET-ENTRY VEHICLES

Once you know whether you're looking at a short-term or long-term endeavor, it's time to consider the various market-entry vehicles. There is a spectrum of choices for selling products internationally that range from domestic-based sales with international destinations to foreign-based sales via your foreign operations.

If you're following a short-term strategy, you'll focus on ways for getting product overseas while relying on your existing domestic relationships and enabling them to manage where the sales wind up. Conversely, if your company considers expansion into a foreign market a long-term growth and diversification play, you are going to take the necessary steps to be on the ground in one way or the other. Your ultimate goal will consist of setting up foreign operations to protect and strengthen your market position.

Let's cover the spectrum of market-entry vehicles, starting with the most temporary short-term play and working up to the most permanent long-term play. Then we'll discuss how the cost, risk, and commitment of these options changes as you move along the spectrum. These three factors will have a big impact on which vehicle is best for your business.

DOMESTIC DISTRIBUTOR WITH INTERNATIONAL SALES

The first short-term option is a domestic distributor selling your product internationally. The process is simple. Your company sells product to the distributor, who then takes title and ownership of that product and sells it in an international market.

This is a popular option with American companies. For example, there are distributors with operations in Texas that sell products in Mexico, and distributors with outlets in places like Wisconsin and Maine that sell products to Canada.

PIGGYBACK EXPORTING

A subset of dealing with a domestic distributor who sells internationally, "piggyback exporting" occurs when a domestic company with complementary products to yours is selling product internationally but not filling container loads. To be more efficient with their freight, they'll look to ship products of other companies along with theirs.

Piggyback exporting is a win-win. Your company gets a

new sales channel, and the company doing the exporting fills their containers with products like theirs. This setup is like the previous one in that you sell to the exporting company, who takes it from there.

EXPORT MANAGEMENT COMPANIES

A little further along the spectrum is what's referred to as an export management company or an export broker. This is basically a distributor whose specialty is exporting product. They operate in the United States, but their sales are entirely international. For example, there are several export management companies in Miami that focus on Latin America. There are also big companies in San Francisco and Los Angeles that focus on Asia. Like the other two options, you'd make a domestic sale to the export management company, who would then turn around and sell your product to their international customers.

I've worked with export management companies and have had excellent results. The advantage of working with these companies is that you create demand for your product in a new market—thus increasing your sales— without any of the hassles international sales can bring. The downside is that export management companies guard their process from the companies that sell to them. If you want data on the customer base, business contacts, or the logistics involved in shipping your product, you're not going to get it.

Export management companies are a short-term option because they give you an entry point and foreign sales but not long-term building blocks. If you foresee your company's short-term play transitioning into a long-term one, an export management company is probably not the right market-entry vehicle for you. You're ultimately going to struggle if you start with this option and then try to capture that market for yourself.

If your strategy is short-term, however, export management companies can be a great option. Because you're not developing foreign relationships, you won't have to burn bridges. You can simply agree to sell or not sell product. If at some point you cut back what you're selling to the export management company, that may affect their desire to buy from you again, but it doesn't affect your ability to create future opportunities in that market.

INTERNET SALES

When your business has a website, you have international exposure. If you have a product with a value proposition that would resonate in foreign markets, you can consider internet sales as a market-entry vehicle. By selling directly to foreign customers, there would be compliance considerations and shipping logistics to figure out. For small companies shipping overseas via air freight or postal service, the cost to ship can be a stumbling block to selling internationally. But if the product is small enough and the profit margin on those sales covers the cost of shipping, selling via the internet is a viable option.

Internet sales aren't the best long-term strategy because they don't require your company to develop those crucial relationships with foreign sales reps or distributors. That said, it does help your company gauge whether there's a market for your product abroad. You can expand from there if the results are good; you'll just be a little behind the curve.

DOMESTIC BIG-BOX STORES

Toward the middle of the spectrum is the option of selling your product internationally through domestic big-box stores like Walmart that have an international presence. This option straddles the fence in terms of commitment. On one hand, you're using another company to sell to international customers. On the other hand, your company is still responsible for adapting your product to a new market (think labeling and packaging), plus exporting it to the foreign operations of the domestic big-box store you chose.

Dealing with a domestic company during the sales process relieves a lot of headaches, though. For example, if you're working with Walmart, a purchasing agent (likely from Bentonville, Arkansas) will be your main contact. That person will speak English and you won't have to worry about unknown cultural concerns. At the same time, you're not entirely insulated from the foreign side of things. You get some experience shipping product overseas—and can develop relationships around that process—to go with the ease of working with a well-known retailer whose purchasing people are native English speakers.

INDEPENDENT SALES AGENT

You begin to approach the other end of the spectrum when you not only export your product but also sell it through an international business entity. The first international option is known as an independent sales agent. Domestically, we'd call them a manufacturer's rep. This person is not your employee but an independent agent who represents your product to customers internationally and works on a commission basis.

The ideal independent sales agent already reps products that go hand in hand with yours to the people who will be your customers. Think back to our discussion of creating good business relationships and the first quality superior businesspeople possess, which is knowledge of the market and access to customers. Sales agents who are successfully selling complementary products to your target custom-ers have established the connections needed to sell your product, plus their background makes it likely they'll understand your company's value proposition.

I've found that international sales agents also excel at covering dispersed markets. If it's not feasible for you to have separate, salaried sales reps in multiple areas within your market, these agents can adequately cover those areas thanks to their familiarity with customers and their ability to travel to different areas of your market.

I once worked with an independent sales agent who was based in Sydney, Australia, and who covered Southeast Asia for me. What made this arrangement advantageous was that I could deal with someone who spoke English and had a similar cultural affinity as me. Yet when we traveled to different Asian markets, I was able to plug in with the people who became our customers thanks to the sales agent's introductions.

Independent sales agents are also more cost effective than working with a salaried sales rep, because agents only get paid commissions. There are sunk costs, of course, such as business cards, literature, and possible modifications to your website. You will want to go on periodic customer visits with them, so you'll be looking at travel costs on your end. There's also the related cost of providing technical support after the sale of your product. Overall, though, these costs are minimal compared to what you can gain.

The biggest downside to using an independent sales agent is that if they are not fully devoted to your product and your success, there can be some conflicts of interest. They may, for instance, use your product as a loss leader. That is, your product becomes an excuse to stop in or make a sales call. Once they're in front of the customer, the agent will sell your product at a low enough price (potentially taking a loss on it) to get more profitable business from other products they're selling (which may not be yours).

You may also get into conflicts with them about how much energy and time they spend on your product versus the other things they're selling. This means you will have to do your due diligence to select the right independent sales agent.

SALARIED SALES REP

Another solution to the problems associated with independent sales agents is to go a step further and hire a salaried sales rep. This move will give you a full-time person on the ground who is completely devoted to your product. Not only that, they've been trained by your staff to understand and sell your value proposition to customers.

The obvious downside with a salaried sales rep is, well,

they're salaried. No matter the number of sales they make, they're getting paid. Having a foreign employee also means abiding by local employment laws. You're not going to see this rep as much as you'd see a domestic rep, plus, you have the challenges we've discussed related to managing, supervising, and incentivizing someone who's operating half a world away.

There is a relatively new service worth investigating that may help with some of these issues. A professional employer organization (PEO) is a corporate entity set up in a foreign country that's capable of employing people. If you used a PEO, your sales rep would legally be their employee, meaning the PEO would take care of compliance with local employment laws, including pay, benefits, and withholding taxes.

The rep would still be your employee, however, for the purposes of training, supervision, direction, reporting, and other matters related to your company. Instead of paying the sales rep a salary directly, your company would pay the PEO a contract rate comprised of both the sales rep's salary and benefits, plus the profit portion for the PEO.

FOREIGN DISTRIBUTOR

Going a step further, you could use a foreign distributor. This may mean a contractual relationship with the foreign distributor and no employees of your own abroad, or you may have a local sales rep who supports the sales to this distributor.

Working with a foreign distributor is a long-term strategy that can take your international efforts to the next level. For one thing, a distributor enables you to ship larger quantities. They can break shipments down and get smaller quantities to customers, which is helpful if your sales are growing but none of your customers need a container-load of product.

Another advantage of using a foreign distributor is that, like distributors in the United States, they will frequently have their own sales force and technical support staff. This will essentially make them your hands and feet on the ground.

You will have some things to consider before you start working with a foreign distributor, though. These include licensing trade names and trademarks so the distributor can use them correctly to market your product. One key to successfully managing these relationships is to become involved with and supportive of their work. For example, you should attend trade shows together, ensuring that the distributor is effectively representing your company and your product.

FOREIGN OPERATIONS

The entry vehicle with the most permanence is a foreign operation. This is when your company forgoes exporting altogether and either purchases or builds facilities in a country to make and source your product. We'll discuss the options for a foreign operation in a moment, but many companies choose to go this route to make their international efforts more localized. For example, maybe you're selling in Asia and you open a plant in China, Malaysia, or another country that is focused on fabricating your product. Or maybe you simply want to support your market presence by having a more local operation.

IMPACT OF COST, RISK, AND COMMITMENT

As you move along the spectrum, the market-entry vehicles become more expensive, riskier, and require a greater time investment. Building a plant in your new market can cost millions, whereas working with a domestic distributor who sells internationally involves virtually no extra cost. Hiring foreign employees is more expensive than having your local sales rep pick up the phone and call the export management company.

As you move along the spectrum, you will also increase the difficulty of exit. It takes a lot more to shut down a foreign operation, or even terminate a relationship with a foreign distributor or a foreign employee, than to simply decide not to sell as much product to a domestic customer who may then sell the product abroad.

The foreign documentation and regulatory requirements we've discussed in previous chapters will become more complex as you move toward long-term strategies. Not to mention, the time horizon of your commitment will be proportionally greater the further you move toward setting up operations in a foreign market.

The increased cost, complexity, and time commitment of long-term entry vehicles mean your company is taking a greater risk the further you move along the spectrum. But if you do things correctly, you're also looking at a more significant return on investment. That's why if your aim internationally is strategic growth and business development, you should consider vehicles that allow you to develop the necessary foreign relationships.

SPECTRUM OF POSSIBILITIES

SHORT TERM (Low Cost/Low Risk/Low Return)							LONG TERM (Higher Cost/Higher Risk/Higher Return)	
Distributor w/ Int'l Sales	Piggyback Exporting	Export Mgmt Co.	Internet Sales	Domestic Big Box	Indep. Sales Agent	Sales Rep	Foreign Distributor	Foreign Operations
Costs ⟶								
Difficulty of Exit Strategies ⟶								
Documentation and Regulation ⟶								
Time Horizon for Commitment ⟶								

Positive Correlation Between the Time, Risk, and Return

Note that all but the most permanent entry vehicle—foreign operations—involve a contractual arrangement. You will have a contract, for example, with your domestic distributor or your export management company. If you're working with an independent sales agent or salaried sales rep, you'll have a sales or employment contract with them.

We've looked at ways in which to structure these deals so they're mutually beneficial, but the beauty of contracts in this context is their impermanence. Deals expire, and while it's harder to fold up shop the further you move along the spectrum, it's possible to plan an exit strategy that doesn't burn bridges or waste resources if ownership isn't involved.

If the best move for your company is establishing foreign operations, you've got two main structures to consider: a joint venture (JV) and a wholly owned foreign enterprise (WOFE). Let's look at the pros and cons of both options, starting with a JV.

PARTNER UP TO CREATE A JOINT VENTURE

A JV is formed when two or more businesses combine to make a new, front-end business entity. A JV agreement is, unto itself, a contract. However, instead of merely having a contractual relationship, you and your partners are now co-owners of a new legal entity that you can use to make and market your product in another country. Some countries require that foreign companies operate in conjunction with a domestic partner, thus necessitating the formation of a JV. Even if it's not legally required, JVs can be a viable option for companies looking to do business internationally.

That said, some JVs work better than others. Factors such as chemistry, team dynamics, management structure, supervision setup, and division of costs and profit will determine how well a JV does and how long it lasts. The essential quality that successful JVs have is that the partners possess complementary strengths.

For example, a company that is terrific at product design and can skillfully position it for sales and marketing might partner with a company capable of producing that product at a cost low enough that it can deliver in a new market on a large scale. The combination of manufacturing and logistics with sales, marketing, design, and branding would in theory position this JV for mutual, long-term success.

It's a recipe for disaster when both parties have the same strengths, as there's likely to be constant conflict over which party's approach to manufacturing, for example, is best for the JV. This is just one reason that JVs tend to last about five to ten years.

Quite often, a JV will end when one or both parties decide they could be more successful on their own. Sometimes a JV is doomed from the start because of bad chemistry between the partners. Disagreements about management style or how decisions are made stand in the way of the teamwork that leads to a strong relationship and a win-win situation.

Poor management can also cause a JV to fall apart. Being a separate entity, a JV typically has a board of directors and management personnel. If the people assigned to those positions don't have the cultural acuity needed to effectively work with partners in another cultural context, the partnership isn't going to function for long. I've seen a JV fall apart because an American company chose the wrong representative to work with its Chinese partner. Too much miscommunication, as well as a lack of trust, led to a swift demise.

To have a successful JV, look for partners that share your company's goals and bring complementary skills to the table. When all parties know the finish line and what they're doing to get there, a JV can be a beneficial arrangement for all those involved.

GOING ALL THE WAY WITH A WOFE

At the far end of the spectrum is the most permanent

market-entry vehicle: a wholly owned foreign enterprise, or WOFE. This is a foreign operation that your company fully owns and operates. When planning to establish a WOFE, you will need to understand the legal requirements and environment of the market you want to enter. In some countries, it is against the law for a foreign company to establish a WOFE, as there will need to be some domestic ownership involved, even if it's just a 10-percent stake. Most countries, however, allow companies to establish and operate a WOFE without domestic involvement.

Your company has two options when establishing a foreign-based operation: acquiring an existing operation or building one from scratch, which is called a green-field operation. When weighing these options, among your considerations should be your company's history of developing operations and the nature of your new market's regulatory environment. If you see red flags with both issues, it might be best to acquire an existing operation.

One of the advantages of acquiring an existing operation is that you will have a facility right away. You will probably keep at least some of the employees because they have useful experience. The downside to purchasing an existing operation is that you may wind up with employees you'd rather not have, and in some jurisdictions, it's difficult to terminate them. You may also realize that the facility is not up to your standards in terms of workplace safety or environmental performance and compliance.

If you go with a greenfield operation, you'll get to build the exact facility your company needs and hire the people you want to work in it. The downside is that in any country, acquiring property, owning property, obtaining building permits, and building a new facility can be complicated and take much longer than expected. You will have to wade through these complications from half a world away while dealing with a different cultural context. You get greater control with a greenfield operation, but most of the time, it ends up being the more expensive and complicated route to go.

The following diagram summarizes the varying structures you can use to implement an international business plan, from contractual relationships to ownership of foreign operations.

BUSINESS STRUCTURES

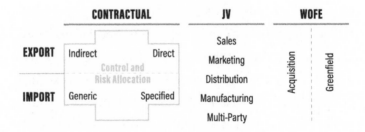

NEW CHALLENGES AND KEY CONSIDERATIONS

Whatever market-entry vehicle you choose, success in a new market will bring challenges you might not expect. One we've discussed already is that when your product is selling well, a local company will eventually create a competitive product and sell it for much less. For global companies like Coca-Cola that have a robust export position, strong patents, trademarks, and powerful brand recognition, this is less of a concern.

But if your product is generic or has no brand name or recognition, cheaper alternatives pose a serious problem. I've had this happen to me, and the results can be shocking. Your local market can get cut in half overnight. That's why it's essential to anchor your company and its products in your new market before potential competitors become real competitors. You typically have a window of three years or so before this happens, but planning should start long before then. As you're researching new markets, gathering on-the-ground intel, and preparing to get your company export-ready, this needs to be part of the discussion.

One way to establish a strong foothold is to develop relationships with the right foreign partners, those people and organizations that you can trust and that will help you be successful thanks to their knowledge, connections, and understanding of your product and its value. As you consider the various market-entry vehicles, keep in mind how your relationships will evolve as part of your short-term or long-term plan. For example, you may start out in a contractual distribution relationship, but once an opportunity for growth presents itself, you might consider forming a JV with that partner.

As you form these relationships, ask yourself if this partner can grow with you.

Proper planning also applies to budgeting. If your goal is to acquire a foreign company or develop a greenfield operation in the future to protect your market position, you need to incorporate a capital budgeting strategy into your export plan to enable your longer-term goals to become a reality.

Even if you start with a short-term play, always think ahead and strategize about the kind of people to work with, what skill sets are needed, and how you can grow the capital needed to one day acquire an operation in this market. That's not to say your company has to transition a short-term play into a long-term commitment, but if a golden opportunity presents itself in your new market, you don't want to miss out by default. That requires planning so your company is ready with a plan and the necessary resources.

CONCLUSION

Entering a new market is in some ways like starting a new business, and you need to treat it as such. Keep the following things in mind, and you're far more likely to succeed.

✿ **Plan with intention.** When you begin this step in growing your organization, draw up a business plan for this new venture. Understand your product and value proposition and how you're going to successfully deliver both to your customers. Know who your customers are, where they live, and how you can reach them.

✿ **Determine your strategy.** Decide in advance whether entering this new market is a short-term or long-term play, and plan accordingly. As we've seen, both are legitimate, but they involve different choices and consequences. If you don't know the scope of your efforts, you risk burning bridges with your foreign partners.

- **Be willing to devote yourself to this expansion.** You will need to be patient and committed to developing good relationships in new cultural contexts. If you take time to learn about different cultures, I think you'll find the process enjoyable. I always did. Commit to becoming fluent, not necessarily in another language, but at least in another cultural context, so you can avoid faux pas and foster positive relationships with overseas contacts and be successful in your negotiations.
- **Be open to new experiences.** This new venture is an adventure in many ways. You will be eating unusual food and sitting through long airplane rides. You will be navigating in taxicabs through unfamiliar streets with signs you can't read. Look at these experiences not as obstacles to overcome but as opportunities for growth.
- **Be flexible.** You have planned this expansion with a mission in mind. There are measurable results you want to achieve. Keep in mind, however, that results are dependent not just on you but also on your customers and sales partners. This is where cultural understanding comes in. You may arrive at your goals differently than you expected. Keep an open mind and be flexible if that happens.
- **Don't forget to ask, "What's in it for me?"** Look at this question not only from your perspective but also from the perspective of your foreign partners. Make sure your interests are aligned so that when you win,

they win. Shared goals and mutual success will keep all parties pulling in the same direction.

- ✿ **Act ethically.** Superior businesspeople act ethically. There are no loopholes or exceptions to this rule. Avoid the lure of corruption and act with decency. In doing so, you will attract the kind of people who act the same way. Not only is acting ethically a moral issue; it's also a practical one. It will help you avoid legal problems at home and in the country where you're doing business. It will ensure you can trust your business contacts and help you sleep at night.

THE LAST GREAT HOPE OF HUMANKIND

After years of working in this field, I can say with complete sincerity that I believe international business is the last great hope of humankind.

You hear about conflict and political discord around the world, and politicians and governments talking about each other like we're on the verge of war. But if you do business around the world, it doesn't matter where you are going; you will find people with common concerns. We're all trying to make a living and do what's needed to support our families. We're trying to build something that will leave the next generation better off.

Essentially, we all speak a common language.

Spend enough time in the world of international business and you'll find yourself not only sharing dinners with gracious people, but you'll also get invited to their home to break bread with their family. It makes you realize that the world is built on our personal relationships. Through these, you find your common humanity.

Everything that goes into international business makes me cynical about governments and politicians but also optimistic about humanity. Take the United States and China, for example. If you look at the relationships formed between American and Chinese businesspeople, you'll find that's where our strength and abilities lie. Despite our countries being opposed on so many issues and the heated rhetoric that results from this, our mutual prosperity, as well as those personal connections, ultimately keep us from serious conflict.

International business impacts people in other ways as well. Its role in the well-being of people in countries around the world is enormous. Think back to the miracle of the Chinese economy from chapter 3. When I first visited China in the mid-1990s, the population was about 1.2 billion. Of those 1.2 billion, about 100 million people lived a somewhat middle-class, financially secure life. The other 1.1 billion people lived in abject poverty.

In China today, there are about eight hundred million

financially secure, middle- or upper-class citizens. China alone has raised seven hundred million people from dollar-a-day poverty to a financially secure existence simply by doing one thing: they opened their country to international business and trade. I would challenge anyone to show me a government program or nongovernmental organization that transformed the daily lives of that many people.

With the gifts that international business can bestow on people around the globe, we as businesspeople have a responsibility to undertake our endeavors with careful planning and consideration for all parties involved. It's not just about companies making a quick buck in a foreign market and then jumping ship. International business is about exploring new opportunities and building relationships that improve the lives of all those involved.

That might be a sentimental, overly optimistic belief, but I'd like to think that business, when shared among the cultures of the world, can bring out the best in us.

TAKING THE NEXT STEP

When you add up everything we've discussed in this book, taking your business to a foreign market might feel like an overwhelming proposition. To that I would say, "Don't limit yourself. If other organizations can do this, why not yours?"

My journey started when I was tasked with turning around a struggling operation our company had in Mexico. Remember, I had zero international business experience at the time! I wish I had known some of the lessons I've shared in this book before I started. I learned these truths the hard way—through trial and error and making more mistakes than I can count. What I learned, above all else, is the power of preparation.

Aside from reading this book and implementing the strategies we've covered, you can prepare by getting involved with the international business community that exists in your area. Consider becoming a member of your local World Trade Center and get to know other businesspeople involved in international business. In doing so, you'll learn a great deal about international business and networking with people who can lend guidance. You'll also sharpen your mindset by surrounding yourself with open-minded people, which is crucial for success with any endeavor, business or otherwise.

I've also included an appendix that lists helpful resources, many of which were mentioned throughout the book. I don't want this to be the last book you read on international business, so I've included some suggested titles you'll want to check out.

If you'd like to work together, I enjoy speaking to groups

of businesspeople who are looking to make a difference in their organizations and in the world. I would be happy to discuss speaking engagements or opportunities for corporate training. You can see the services I offer, and you can contact me personally. My website is www.exin-globalstrategies.com.

To close, I'd like to offer one final reminder: Don't go it alone. Trying to take your business international without help is the quickest way to screw things up. Get the help you need and never lose sight of your goal. The path you take to get there may be unpredictable and challenging at times, but it's an adventure that will ultimately grow not only your business but also your knowledge of the world, other people, and yourself.

REFERENCES AND RESOURCES

The following websites, journal articles, and books are recommended for doing initial market research, diving deeper into the details necessary to execute a market-entry strategy, and gaining a more profound understanding of the global environment in which we do business.

WEBSITES

globalEDGE (https://globaledge.msu.edu). Terrific website full of economic data, trade statistics, and other fact-based information on most countries and economic regions in the world.

Export.gov (https://www.export.gov/welcome). The website of the US Department of Commerce dedicated to helping American companies succeed as exporters.

World Trade Center Denver (https://www.wtcdenver. org). The WTC in Denver offers a regular schedule of real-world practical business training seminars and other programs designed to help companies make the most of their international opportunities. A number of its offerings are also available as online courses and webinars that can be accessed from anywhere.

NationMaster (http://www.nationmaster.com/statistics). Extremely helpful website for getting at granular market data, such as the number of hospital beds in a country or the number of people with access to personal computers in a given market.

CIA *World Factbook* (https://www.cia.gov/library/pub-lications/the-world-factbook). An excellent source for information on macro-economic statistics as well as insights on economic and political risk factors. A report is available for most countries in the world.

China Law Blog (https://www.chinalawblog.com). Dan Harris and his colleagues at the Harris Bricken law firm in Seattle have been blogging about China since 2006, and their blog contains some of the most astute and helpful insights into the legal, cultural, and business environ-ments in China that you will find anywhere on the web.

Going Global Blog (http://exinglobal.typepad.com/

going_global). This is my blog on international business launched in 2006. I have not been as consistent a blogger as I might have been, but if you found *Go Glocal* to be helpful, you may find other useful insights on both big-picture and small-picture topics related to international business, as well as any updates in my thinking and experiences yet to come.

JOURNAL ARTICLES

"**Emerging Giants: Building World-Class Companies in Developing Countries,**" Tarun Khanna and Krishna G. Palepu, *Harvard Business Review*, October 2006. This is the article mentioned in the book from which I first gained the insight into the four levels of a market, which you need to understand to know where your business will fit.

"**How Competitive Forces Shape Strategy,**" Michael E. Porter, *Harvard Business Review*, March 1979. This is the original article in which Professor Porter discusses his Five Forces, which are referred to in the book as a means to understand your competitive environment. He has written and spoken about this topic many times since, including updating his original thesis in subsequent *Harvard Business Review* articles, but this was the beginning.

BOOKS

The Global Entrepreneur: Taking Your Business International, **4th ed.,** by James F. Foley (Jamric Press International, 2017). Originally published in 1999, Jim Foley's book remains an essential desk reference on all the nuts and bolts of exporting successfully. Anyone attempting to sell product internationally should keep a copy of this book close at hand.

Kiss, Bow, or Shake Hands: The Bestselling Guide to Doing Business in More than 60 Countries, **2nd ed.,** by Terri Morrison and Wayne A. Conaway (Adams Media, 2006). A great reference book to consult before traveling to a new country, as it neatly summarizes key aspects of business culture and the tricky dos and don'ts of body language and what's considered polite in sixty different countries.

All Marketers Are Liars (Tell Stories): The Underground Classic that Explains How Marketing Really Works—and Why Authenticity Is the Best Marketing of All, **reprint ed.,** by Seth Godin (Portfolio, 2012). I recommend this in the book as a place to take a deeper dive into the critical concept of a business's value proposition. If you're in business, this is a book (along with Godin's other wonderful books on marketing and business creation) that you owe it to yourself to read.

What the CEO Wants You to Know: How Your Com-

pany Really Works, **expanded and updated ed.,** by Ram Charan (Currency, 2017). Only 176 pages but very likely the best single book on business fundamentals ever written. Charan is the person who taught me the power of Return = Margin x Velocity in analyzing the dynamic nature of a business's performance.

Boomerang: Travels in the New Third World, by Michael Lewis (Norton, 2011). Michael Lewis is the most gifted financial writer out there, and this irreverent recounting of the unfolding of the 2008 economic crisis is a wonderful place to begin to understand the interconnectivity of global business and finances.

The Travels of a T-Shirt in the Global Economy: An Economist Examines the Markets, Power, and Politics of World Trade, **2nd ed.,** by Pietra Rivoli (Wiley, 2014). Following the manufacture and sale of a T-shirt from the growing of the cotton in Texas to its manufacture in textile mills in China to its ultimate sale in a secondhand clothing stall in Africa, this is one of the best books I've ever read on global economics and the interweaving of international business and government policy. As good a place as any to start to gain critical insight into the world in which you are about to be doing business.

Ted Levitt on Marketing, by Ted Levitt (Harvard Business Review Books, 2006). This is a collection of a number of

Professor Levitt's writings on marketing and business and, importantly for this purpose, includes his seminal article from the *Harvard Business Review* titled, "The Globalization of Markets," which popularized the notion of globalization as a phenomenon that all businesspeople need to pay attention to and understand.

ACKNOWLEDGMENTS

To my friends and colleagues from my time at Johns Manville, all wonderful, dedicated, inspiring people. But most especially Dixon Walker, who took a gamble and launched me into a career in international business, and Jerry Henry, our then-CEO, who, in reply to a brief report on performance and metrics, simply asked, "What I really want to know is, are you learning?" I'm happy to say that I learned a great deal, and I hope the reader learned something valuable from this book.

To my many friends and fellow international business enthusiasts with whom I have been involved through the World Trade Center Association in Denver over the past twenty-five years. I learned a lot from being able to trade stories and experiences with a group of people so dedicated and passionate about international travel, trade, and culture. Especially Jim Reis and Karen Gerwitz, who in their respective tenures as president of WTC Denver had the vision and commitment to build it into what I believe is the premier international business resource in the country. Many of the themes in this book were developed in teaching training courses and making presentations to business groups through WTC Denver.

To the many students whom I have had the pleasure and privilege of teaching through the EMBA program at Colorado State University and the College of Business at Johnson & Wales University in Denver. Their enthusiasm, curiosity, and questions have kept me on my toes and ensured that I continue to learn and grow myself. I am especially grateful to those who enjoyed the classes so much that they said, "I wish you'd write a book about all this." This book isn't about everything we covered, but it's a start. I would be remiss not to mention one student in particular, Brittney Martinson, now a success in her own right, traveling the globe helping other businesses grow and develop. She not only told me I should write a book, but she kept pushing me until I actually did.

To the great team at my publisher, especially Tom Lane who helped immensely in getting my ideas organized, Josh Raymer who made sure the words got out of my head and onto paper, and Coleen Jamison and Katherine Sears who oversaw the whole process and ultimately produced the book that is in your hands.

To my brother Bob, who has been cheering me on since, well, since forever. Enough to say he's the best big brother one could ask for.

To my daughters Aryanna and Alison, always keeping me on my toes, always in my heart. I love you both.

To my dad who, even though he passed away a few years ago, remains my hero and whose voice I still hear in my head whenever I'm faced with a difficult problem to resolve.

Last but by no means least, to my mother, who, when I was young, gave me a book of blank pages, telling me it was for me to "write whatever it is that you write." Creative thinking is a key to problem solving, and in that simple gesture, my mother nurtured my creative energy, which now fills a book of more than just blank pages.

ABOUT THE AUTHOR

 **CRAIG MAGINNESS** has worked for the past decade as the managing member of ExIn Global Strategies, which advises businesses looking to grow into new markets. Craig spent much of his career at a Fortune 1000 company, overseeing international operations, directing sales and marketing, and serving as president of two of the company's foreign subsidiaries. An adjunct professor at Johnson & Wales University, he also served as president and chairman of the World Trade Center Denver, where he has trained entrepreneurs, company executives, and trade support specialists to be more successful international business people. In 2013, he was named "International Trade Educator of the Year" by NASBITE International.